Lessons

By Michelle LaVigne-Wedel
with Alex

Edited by: Paul Wedel

Sweetgrass Press
P.O. Box 1862
Merrimack NH 03054

Library of Congress Cataloging-in Publication Data
Michelle LaVigne-Wedel. 1962-

Library of Congress Card Number: 00-191447

Lessons / Michelle LaVigne-Wedel
with Alex

ISBN 0-9702630-2-3

COVER DESIGN: The Electric Wigwam

Printed in the United States of America

Address all inquiries:
Sweetgrass Press
P.O. Box 1862
Merrimack, NH 03054-1862

Table of Contents

Foreword

During the past few years, I have learned a lot about myself. Including a gift I have for "hosting" other beings — or, as some would put it, Channeling.

As anyone who knows me, or read anything I have written, know, I am not — and never have been— a fan of channeling. Even to this day, I prefer to call it "the C word" as if it is a bad word. I have not had good experiences with people I have met who have claimed to channel. With two exceptions, I was totally sure from the very start that all the people who "channeled" for me were either (at best) projecting their higher self, or, (at worst) straight out lying to me. I must note that the two exceptions were outstanding experiences.

Still, the idea of channeling was something I would rather not have dealt with, especially publicly where I would not only be open to criticizim, but worse yet, lumped in with the fakes and misguided who claim to channel. The idea of talking in public, nevermind writing a book, had me terrified. It seemed the ETs had different ideas.

By the mid 1990's I was begining to believe I was loosing my mind. I would sit at my computer to do some typing or maybe play a video game, and suddenly be aware that my monitor was showing me pages and pages of information that I had no memory of writing. I also noticed time had passed.

One day, I was reading what "magically appeared"

on my screen and found the word "supraliminal". I am a bit embarrassed to say it, but I did not know what the word meant. I sat there wondering how I could have written a word I did not even know. I looked it up in the dictionary. It was a real word. Furthermore, it was used in the correct context. I didn't know what to make of all this. By and large, I kept it a secret.

After my work with my husband, Paul, started, and we began to have open contact through me with various forces from the Earth, I realized there was a bigger purpose for all this. Alex explained he wrote the text I found on my computer. I then agreed to let him take the time to finish what he started out to do. So the book you hold became a reality.

The following "Lessons" have come directly from a being named Alex. These are the same lessons he teaches in the ET world.

Both Paul and I have found tremendous significance and value in these lessons. Though we both have to admit, some of the concepts took several readings and a lot of inner thinking to understand. I have found that many of the lessons have a far deeper meaning inside than they appear to have on the surface. Paul and I continue to find new truths and concepts each time we read them. We hope you find value in them as well.

Remember as you read the following, they were not written by me. Please do not feel slighted when Alex refers to you as "child". This is a common way many of these beings address humans.

In order to make sure we did not change the meanings, Paul and I did not remove, add or change the presentation of the information at all.

I am sure, like the two of us, you will find meaning every time you read these lessons. Also like us, I would not be surprised if you read them again and again.

To Begin

Stop and pause for a moment. Look at where you are in this existence and evaluate your direction. Don't move. Don't explain. Just reflect. Are you exactly where you believe you should be at this point? Are you pleased with your progress within this mission? Is your direction sound?

Look at the course of your travels. Look at the pace at which you are taking your steps. Often, you may feel you are moving too slowly to reach your goal. But I say to you, stop. Rush not ahead only to lose your direction, rather, move steadily. Fear not that you are going to be late. You will be there in time, just as you are expected to be. There is no true limit to the amount of time you have at your command. You will do this. We know, because you have before, and you will once again.

Know that the rhythm of the pace in your head is one that you dance to every day. You may interpret it very differently at different times, but it never changes, only your way of hearing it changes. Your mission is constant. Its rhythm is unchanging. Its speed does not fluctuate. It is as uniform as the pulsing of the stars you draw your energy from. You are filled with the rhythm of the universe; the rhythm of existence. It is your nature and the nature of all things eternal. It is your song.

Do not deny your nature. Listen to its symphony and dance to it. Pause now and listen to the rhythms of your own soul and know that this is the beating of the universal heart. Feel it in your hands, your feet, your body, your being. It is all you really are; a wonderful note in the song of the universe. Be not afraid to sing! You must sing! Without your note, the song is not complete.

Be a servant to the rhythm of the universe and it will serve you well. Be always aware of it. Be always in time with it, and you will have no fear of being late. Sing your note to eternity, and you will hear the complete song.

For the tone that you are is not important in itself. It is just a sound. It is just a passing vibration of the rhythm. But when in its proper place, the tone that is you, is a necessary piece of perfection. Only as part of the whole, are you truly alive. Only as part of the song, is a note anything but noise.

Remember this. It is important

The Nature of Knowledge

Child, you read this for that golden gift so far from all you touch. You require knowledge. By your birth nature, you are inquisitive, but this is not enough. Just to be curious is not a prerequisite to attaining the kind of knowledge you are seeking. For knowledge is a power far beyond the grasp of most children. You do not teach your offspring how to light a match before they respect fire. Why? Because this, like all knowledge, brings with it power. In this instance it is the power to create fire; a power the child does not comprehend. It is a power that is dangerous in his hands.

All knowledge, no matter how useless it seems to you, is a key to some power somewhere. What this power is may be evident or it may not be. But once you control the key, you have to decide to use it and hope you can control the results; or ignore it, and block it from your life mind, and continue as if the knowledge was never presented to you.

Often, your mission depends on what you do with the knowledge you acquire in your journey. That is why knowledge is such an awesome responsibility. For once you know something, you must choose to act on it, even if it is to ignore it and do nothing.

To know what knowledge truly is, is important. You must understand what a thing is before you can dissect its parts and look at each of the pieces. If you do what you have a history of doing, you will look at the parts of a thing and try to assemble it from the pieces. This is time consuming and often leads you to incomplete or incorrect views of the whole. So much easier it is to look at the whole and then take it apart in a carefully ordered way. Then you can understand each part and how it relates to the completed whole.

Many parts have no meaning unless you look at their relationship to the completed object, concept or truth. When you are faced with such a piece, child, you may find yourself assigning a meaning to that piece that is inappropriate. You do this because it is difficult for you to conceive that the piece is nothing when taken by itself, with no reference to the whole. Many of the answers you are looking for concern the various interpretations of some of these pieces.

Knowing — in this existence — is the act of becoming aware of something or some truth. It is not the act of *learning* something or some truth. You do not need to learn anything. You already have all truths inside of you. You already have all answers to all questions imprinted in the rhythm of your soul.

Remember, child, you are not just what you seem to be. Though from your isolated state of life, you are often very confused and unsure, you are in fact complete and perfect. We will discuss this in more depth later. Be content at this point, to know that this is true.

Because of the limits you have taken on in order to exist in this state of life, you cannot encompass the total of what you are at any one Earth-time. The vessel you have to maintain in order to be part of the Earth is far too limited to allow you to be complete. You have, in order to become part of this Earth-life, left much of yourself and your tools behind. Most of you regret your choice of what you took and what you left behind. By your nature, you will feel that you often need the very thing you did not take with you.

But this is only illusion. You have what you need. Do not let yourself feel bitter because *all* your knowledge was not among the tools you could take.

Most of you did have access to more knowledge when you were new to this world, but the circumstance of your Earth-life caused you to be fearful of using this knowledge. You allowed others to make you believe it was wrong or evil and you locked it away from yourself. You may have believed you were protecting yourself. That was probably correct at the time, but as conditions changed, you did not release the knowledge. There is likely no good reason for you to forbid yourself access to it any longer.

Unlocking this stored knowledge is easier than you think. Just give yourself the permission to hear it again. It is still there.

Accessing the knowledge you are storing outside this Earth-life, in true reality, is another task which is more difficult. Often, it has to be done on a "time sharing" basis with other knowledge you have in your "toolbox." To have admittance to all of what you truly know at once would make it impossible to exist in this Earth-life. You must continue to exist here until your mission is complete.

For this reason, the truth — the knowledge if you prefer — is portioned out to you in small sections. Though we find it difficult, we know you cannot have a complete understanding. At any one time, therefore, we strive to give you the pieces that have meaning on their own. Our hope is that you can apply them to the whole, and with the direction of the consciousness leading you, you will make the correct assessment of each part and eventually the correct assessment of the whole.

There are things happening to your Earth body to make it more useful a tool for the storage of knowledge. You may even be aware of these things, though you probably do not understand them. We will discuss them in a coming lesson.

Once you are aware that something is true, you are responsible for keeping the truth pure and exposing those around you to that truth, so they may also have the opportunity to absorb it and teach it to others.

Knowledge is only a state of awareness. What is commonly called knowledge in this Earth-life is only a collection of truths. Sometimes non-truths are misunderstood as knowledge. The test of whether knowledge is actual truth or mislabeled non-truth is whether the fact presented is eternal. Since truth is eternal, so is knowledge. If knowledge is perceived to be complete and ended, it is not knowledge at all. If you can know everything about anything in this Earth-life, then you know nothing about it at all. For what you believe is knowledge is just a collection of misguided facts and thoughts. You cannot *know* everything in your present Earth-life state. We are careful in choosing the words *misguided facts*. For as you know, my child, there is some truth in everything that is considered knowledge. Often, it is just the limits we put on the truths that cause them to become invalid.

The concept of life is an excellent example of this. Many Earthers are aware that their lives are eternal. This is a truth. But they limit their concepts of what eternity is to a uni or bi-directional timeline of measured Earth existence. By imposing this limitation, they have lost the pure meaning of that simple truth. So, it is in this frame of understanding the concept of eternal life is no longer truth.

Are you, child, eternal? Yes. Are you eternal explained in the constrictions of the accepted human concept of eternity, that being linear time unending? No, you are so much more than that. You are literally more than you can imagine in this Earth-life. Much more.

There are some pieces of knowledge that are physical plane based specific. These are truths that hold to all the physical plane, but are not complete or not even valid when taken out of the physical plane. One plus one will always equal two on Earth, but it means nothing in reality.

Child, before I begin to unfold knowledge to you, I must make you aware that what I am about to say will often coincide with what you know already. It will confirm things you have been made aware of from several other teachers and from your own toolbox of insight. This will not be a problem for you. Where you may find difficulty with what I say, will be when the things I say do not seem to fit with what others who have spoken in this medium before have said.

This is, in almost all cases, because we all have different parts of the picture to unfold for you — different pieces of the truth I spoke of earlier. It is imperative that you understand this concept. Just as it takes many notes to make the song of the universe, it takes many pieces of truth to assemble the total of knowledge. No part of the truth is wrong, though it may be wrong for your piece of the puzzle. It may not fit in your personal toolkit. For this reason, it is not expected of you to make all things part of your heart song. What you do not need you will not absorb, so you do not need to worry about it. If you try and force yourself to absorb things that do not fit, you will only become confused and your mind will be filled with noise. You must not let that happen. If what you labor to absorb is meant for your toolkit, do not fight it. It will, in time come to you, and you will all at once be aware of it. Remember, you are not trying to *learn* anything. You are trying to *awaken* things you already hold dormant.

If all teachers revealed the same truths, all children would hold identical pieces of knowledge. I admit, this would make the job of the teachers so much easier because the children would have no reason to question beyond the small slice of truth they all possess. Their siblings would be holding identical pieces. There would be no conflict between the children who hold different pieces. There would be no jealousy between children who envy the knowledge the other possesses. There would be not one of you, child, who believes she needs to know so much more and so much faster to be worthy of her mission. These are all things that cause your teachers great sadness. We would like to see them gone.

But if you, child, had an identical piece as all the other children you are destined to work with, you would be useless. The universal song would be noise if it had only one note that kept repeating with no pattern or reason. The song cannot be complete without a complement of notes, as knowledge cannot be complete without a complement of truths. So, if you come across teachers imparting information from the same source that are seemingly opposed, take time to reflect upon them. I am sure you will find they are often different sides of the same coin. You will find, I am certain, that they are just different pieces of the greater puzzle. Or maybe, they are the same truths explained in terms more complex or simple than your understanding. This too happens.

You, child, are part of vast, intricate network of other mission workers woven into this Earth-life. You are, in whole, far greater than the sum of each of you individually. You are always connected, though you do not have full awareness of this. You are like the vines of a thick forest or the threads of a complex web. If one is touched, all are touched. The progress one makes, all will benefit from. Because of this interaction, you constantly become aware of and unaware of knowledge possessed by other children. You can access this network as you need to. In this way, you can retrieve knowledge you need quickly, without the overload of information that would cease your existence on this Earth.

Much like the computer system I am using to convey this concept to you, the knowledge that you access from this network is not permanent. You can, of course, choose to keep the information if you have room in your toolkit for it. But you will, by the nature of your mission, only keep what you need to, in order to do your job with the accuracy demanded of you at the time you accessed this knowledge. There is no room for waste and extras. It is required that you keep your soul as free from noise as can be achieved. Knowledge, and the power it commands, has no place in the tools of one too inexperienced to use it wisely. Matches have no place in a toddler's toy box.

With the experience you are gaining from your Earth-life you will become more confident in when to access your knowledge and when to let situations pass. Do not let your limited knowledge lead you to believe you are the only one who is right at any time. Many different truths can be correct at one time. This is hard to understand in the limited concept of physical truth, nevertheless, it is true.

When you took this mission, you armed yourself with tools such as ego, pride, arrogance, envy and anger. These tools were very necessary to get you to the point in Earth-life were you are now. Do not deny it. All of these negative attributes are in your toolbox. It is the same with all mission workers. These traits were needed to protect you from the crushing effects of physical reality. They were necessary to keep you whole and strong through years of shallow thinking and hollow, unreal people. They helped you survive through friendships and conflicts. They gave you the strength to keep focused when all around you pulled you off center.

These attributes are useful tools when you live like you are merely physical. They are not useful when you want to awaken to your life beyond the confines of this Earth. Now that you have come to the point where you are aware you have a mission in this Earth-life, and you are more than just a resident of Earth. You must let go of these attributes. They will only hold you from awareness and block you from absorbing more pieces of the truth. They are, in other words, taking up needed space in your toolbox.

We know you are aware of this and you are striving to release all negatives. I merely remind. We also know it is hard for you to toss away tools that have served you so well. You will. You have to, in order to make room in your toolbox for more useful tools like knowledge and compassion. Your mission will not succeed without both.

The Mission

Child, your teachers know many of you have heard talk about the mission. We also know few of you are actually aware of what the mission really is. There are many theories among you, based on the partial facts you have. There are many more guesses. The truth about the mission is very complex, yet extremely simple.

To understand it fully, you will need access to knowledge you cannot have in your physical form. Yet, you can get a glimpse of that knowledge through the network in place around you. In order to make it a little easier for you to comprehend, the mission will be laid out to you in a chronological order — which is by no means the best way to describe it. In the future, I will again explain the mission with more emphasis on its truth and less on the confines of linear time.

To start by saying "*in the beginning*" is wrong. There is no beginning. For that matter, there is no ending. There is only *now*. Now is all times. To explain it in linear think, *now is*, *was* and *will be* all at this exact moment. *Now* is all times in one split-second of awareness. *Now* is where you are. *Now* is where we all are in one form or another.

Purely for the sake of a linear think explanation, I will use words that describe time boundaries such as past and future. As you read this relaying of the mission, know this is by far the most imprecise explanation, and therefore, the one most open to misinterpretation. Do not read the following with a preconceived idea of what the words mean. For they can apply incorrectly to many of the myths that prevail on Earth. If you clear your mind of noise and allow your true self to absorb what is written, you are far less likely to distort the facts before you.

Far in the past, consciousness, or rather the song of the universe, perfection, or rather still, God, was. This consciousness was not a person as you understand the concept. It was not an individual. This was not even new to itself. It was, and is, in fact, eternity. It is a living mass. It is changing. It is — in the closest terms you possess— growing. Though this is just a conceptual word since you cannot expand on eternity.

The growth of this consciousness is, in fact, the mission. That is the simple explanation. The method for doing this is a more complex one.

All things physical are created from what you would call energy. Therefore, all physical things are actually pieces of energy in a dormant state. Anything with awareness is a combination of energy in both a physical and a non-physical state. A rock is energy, just as you are. The difference is you have consciousness, therefore you also have a non-physical state. This part has been called the soul. This label can be inappropriate. We will discuss why later as you learn more about the make up of the many bodies you have. (See Lesson 7.)

All things that have energy have a sound — a resonance in the song of the universe. All energy is actually a piece of eternity.

Long ago, this eternity divided into too many pieces for any of us to ever count. It separated into an infinite amount of pieces. Each piece a note of the song. Each piece itself eternal. These are the pieces of true reality.

When the pieces divided, they became things necessary for the growth of the whole. One of the things some of the pieces became was the physical realm. What most Earthers call the universe —the stars, planets and cosmos— is just a collection of a few pieces of this eternity that have become specialized in order to do a particular job for the whole.

The physical aspect of the universe is, therefore, not real in the true sense. It is only an illusion created for a particular purpose. This is a fact many of you may find hard to fit into your toolbox. I will explain what defines reality, and the properties of eternity, in the next lesson. But for the purpose of explaining the mission, know that this is true.

Though the physical universe is not real, the energy that is transformed to create the illusion of the physical universe is real. In small ways, man, by way of his "science", can see this.

The crude method of atomic reaction used in nuclear weapons and power production is an example of how much energy can come from releasing just a small amount of physical elements. Still, both these methods create incredible amounts of semi-unreleased energy in the form of radiation, proving there is even more energy trapped in the "fuel" they could not release. It must dissolve itself away until the balance of energy to physical matter is turned and once again, it becomes dormant.

This simple example illustrates a basic principle that applies to all things. That is, that all things strive for balance. This applies to eternity and all of its parts.

The energy that is eternity is linked together in a vastly complicated mesh of intersecting points that transverses what you would call space, time and dimension. All of these points, joined together, form what could be labeled a "mesh" or "network" of energies. The mesh is a single unit. It is composed of countless parts, but is in fact, one moving, growing consciousness. At any given moment in linear time, each intersection of this mesh is in the process of finding its note, tuning its tone, or achieving harmony with the whole. It is, in other words, at a point of beginning, growing or ending. This is true of all intersections of the mesh at all times. No intersection is free from this cycle.

The beginning of an intersection is that point in reality — not necessarily time or space — that for the purpose of progressing the whole, energies come together and create a joining in the mesh. This intersection does not have to be a planet or a star, as it usually is when it protrudes into the physical. It can be ideas, time or concepts. It can be things you have no words for and no way of understanding within the limits of your toolbox.

Each intersection, once created, has a purpose to fulfill. Sometimes the only purpose of that intersection is to create itself. Most often, the purpose is to add a tone to the song eternal.

The tuning, or growing period of an intersection, (also called a node) in the grid, is that time in the cycle of an intersection when the energies that make it up — each of which has its own distinct sound — tune themselves to each other and create harmony.

The time of ending or of total perfection is that time when the harmony of the intersection is so perfectly in tune with the complete song of the universe it is no longer distinguishable from that song. It has, indeed, merged with perfection. At this point, it is no longer a node. It is now part of the harmony of the total mesh.

These descriptions can be deceptive if you try and make them fit into your linear, logic driven way of life. For in reality, all these phases are happening at the same "time" and every piece of eternity is a perfect eternity in itself. Because of this fact — which many of you may find a paradox — any one individual thing is the total of every other thing, including itself. This does not make sense when you try to fit it into the concepts you are taught by

Earth based theory. Even the adage "the whole is greater than the sum of its parts" does not fit the situation. Actually, in reality, there is no difference from the whole and the part. The only difference you could argue is the function performed by the part and the whole. The work of the whole is to be the mesh, the work of the part is to create the mesh.

There is a pattern to the construction of this mesh that you, child, may find hard to see. It is not simply a series of straight intersecting lines. It is a *dance* of fills and voids. It is a pattern so complex that to look at it from any one point it would look like chaos. The physical make up of the universe is like this. There are vast open spaces between galaxies, and even greater vastness of space between clusters of galaxies. If you could see all the galaxies of the physical universe at one time, you would see the pattern. But from your limited viewpoint, you may not.

Many of you are aware that there is a pattern of energy that encompasses this world. But did you know, child, this whole planet is a physical representation of a node in the energy mesh? It is, in fact, an intersection point of many lines. Some of these lines can be traced back to other intersections in physical space. Others cross out of this physical illusion and into reality, therefore, becoming untraceable by those with physical form.

The intersection of energy you call Earth is in the process of awakening from a dormancy created by a clashing of energy points. It is on the verge of harmonizing all the different energy tones from the different sources that created this intersection.

This can be done in many ways. In the case of Earth, it is being done with the help of a workforce who are laboring to tune the many, many individual energies. Because of a dramatic clash of energies created in the *past,* it became necessary to enlist a workforce to accomplish this synchronization, rather than let "nature take its course". Many unexpected energies of foreign sentience who have altered the frequency of this intersection have to be sorted out in order to complete the harmony that will create the resonance necessary for this intersection to be in agreement with the whole mesh. Once this agreement is achieved, the intersection will resonate with the song of the universe, and the portion of the energy mesh that it maintains will once again be a true part of the whole. All the energy units that are part of this node will find perfection in the eternal song.

Linearly speaking, this re-tuning of the Earth-song is in your *future*. It will be a time of great physical turmoil. For, as you change the frequency of the energy that makes up a thing, you will change that thing. Since the Earth is only energy in physical form, it will physically change as the energies that make it up change. This is only normal and expected.

As we have told you before, child, there will have to be a reconstruction of the energy distribution of this point in the mesh. This reconstruction or re-tuning is what many children have labeled *Earth changes*. Many more have labeled it *the end of the world*. But it is not the end of anything, nor is it the beginning. It is just another season of the universe. It is just another beat in the rhythm of the song.

The whole of the mission from your position, child, is to be a part of this workforce. You are one of the units of energy sent here to help produce this resonance.

So this is the mission. Keep in mind the description of the mission you just read is only the very basic outline of what you can understand using linear think. As you learn more, we will add to this description.

Of Time and Reality

Time is, by most human definitions, a duration of days, seasons, life spans or any particular portion of Earth existence you wish to measure. It is a forward moving calculation that cannot be slowed or stopped. It is a constant in most Earth lives. With the exception of mathematical theory, where it is manipulated by concepts of space and speed, time is an unchanging fact of Earth existence. It controls your Earth-life. It takes count of your every breath and it puts a limit on the time you will exist on Earth. It has, on Earth, become more than just a name for the measuring of days. It has taken on a life of its own. It has a life that is as unreal as anything unreal can be. It is the greatest of the distortions you, child, accept as the truth.

All the energy given to the concept of time has given it a power beyond what is real, even in the context of Earth illusion. Earthers are often heard saying things like "time is a healer" or "time slips through your fingers." With expressions like this, they give a power to time that is not deserved. Remember, only knowledge can bring power. Time has no knowledge and therefore no real power. That is, unless you give it your power.

Mankind is so obsessed with time they have found ways to measure it beyond their ability to comprehend it. Yet all the measuring gives them no control over it. People rush and hurry to beat the clock. People strive to find happiness before they die. People are confused.

The rhythm of the clock is not natural for you. You already have a rhythm in your soul that supersedes any measurement imposed upon you by mankind. Your natural rhythm is more closely linked to the rhythm of the universe than to time.

Since the physical Earth is not eternal it has a finite beginning and ending. When mankind became aware of this, he wished to measure the duration of Earth from beginning to end, thus he had to invent a scale for this. Which he did. He invented the concept of time.

This concept was created to measure an aspect of non-reality, and therefore does not apply outside of the physical plane. If you are some place where there is no beginning or ending and all things are one thing, there is no difference between now, later and before. You have no need to measure that particular dimension of a thing; being "how long will it last". It simply does not apply. Time is not relevant in reality.

The truth, "time is not relevant in reality," is not easy for some children to comprehend. To truly understand it you have to see beyond the concept of linear time. The idea that the events of life happen in a certain order is only true if you are actually physically alive and working in an Earth based frame of reality. Actually, life as you know it on Earth is a grand illusion. It is a dream you take part in so that you may conform to the Earth rhythms and perform your mission.

On Earth, native Earth-life has to progress in a particular sequence in order to advance the natural song of the Earth, thereby fulfilling its mission. You can think of it as a wonderfully complex clockworks with all the cogs turning in perfect order. Each piece doing just what it should do to make the machine run. If left to its own device, Earth would have eventually developed a life form that would — after years of struggle, for the struggle is part of the method — learn the Earth song and help it sing until it was in tune with the rest of eternity. This is the way many physical worlds have progressed.

In the ideal scenario, the supraliminal would eventually know they are the living pieces of a living world. With this knowledge in their toolbox, they would soon develop the ability to access the energy mesh that is eternity. As they progress and strive to touch eternity, they bring their physical world into tune with reality. Eventually they would merge with reality and once again become a conscious part of eternity — a conscious part of God.

There are some basic things to keep in mind when you talk about the universe, time and reality. There are six basic principles that hold true in all the universe. That is, in all reality.

1. Energy is eternal.

It has no beginning or ending in any direction of time, space or dimension. Eternity, as we discussed before, is not just an unending, linear, time-line. It is the total of all things that exist. It never began and will never end. If you searched for all your existence — which would be for all existence for you are eternal — you would never approach a border or outer ring of eternity. It has no outer limits. It is all.

2. If something has an ending, it also has a beginning.

I know this only sounds obvious, but it really can be more than you expect if you think about it. All things that end had a beginning. You cannot be infinite or finite in only one direction. An ending does not necessarily have to be in a *time* direction. It can also be in a space or dimensional direction, as well as directions Earth language has no words to describe. So, if you think of something and know that it does end somewhere or when, then it also began somewhere

19

or when. Likewise, if something has a beginning, it will eventually end. If you can examine a concept or object and know where it began, be assured it has to end.

This is why it is grossly incorrect to start any narrative or explanation of eternity with the words, "*in the beginning.*" There was no beginning and there is no ending. If there was indeed a beginning, then an end is certain.

3. Everything is a perfect reflection of the greater eternity.

Think about this. If you had the ability to take a grand pair of scissors and cut eternity in half, which half would be bigger, the first half of eternity or the second half? If you think you can answer then think again. When you *cut* eternity, did you create a beginning to one half and an end to the other? Or did you create a beginning and an end to both pieces? No, you did neither. I will explain.

For the moment, picture eternity in the form of a linear time-line going off into the future and the past for ever and ever. Imagine you are cutting it at today's date. Now look what you have done. Starting from your cut, does the eternal line go on into the infinite future? Does the other side of the line still go on into the infinite past? True infinity cannot go in only one direction. If either side of your line has no ending or beginning, then you cannot have an ending or a beginning on the other side of the line either. For without beginning there can be no ending.

If you could cut eternity in half, you would have two parts that were also eternal. If you cut it a thousand times, you would have a thousand eternal parts. Further, if you cut it into an infinite number, you would have an infinite number of eternal parts. That is indeed what has happened.

Each part of eternity is an exact replica of all of eternity. Let me explain how we know that. As was illustrated in the previous paragraph, each part of eternity is in itself, eternal. Yet, there can only be one eternity. This is because you cannot — by definition — have anything sitting outside of everything. Therefore, we know what we call individual pieces of eternity are, in fact, the exact same piece of eternity from a different perspective. *All* eternity is *one* eternity. And though any piece of eternity you inspect may seem unique, it is an exact replica of the whole.

4. All things are perfect and complete in their design.
        How can anything be less than complete if it is eternal? Those things which are real are the total of everything, they have nothing missing. If they did they would not be eternal, and therefore, not real.

5. Everything in reality has a complement.
        The fact that anything real is actually the total of everything eternal leads to something you may find as a paradox from your current physical point of view. That being, everything in reality —which is, as you know, anything eternal — has a complement. This complement is totally and completely opposite in every way and detail to the original. Moreover, everything is identical to its complement in every way and detail. There is no difference between a piece of reality and its total opposite. For both the *subject* and its *opposer* are reflections of the same eternity.

6. Nothing in reality will remain the same.
        Everything in reality is continually in the process of becoming. If a "thing" in reality ever completed its journey of growth, it would have an ending, and therefore it would not have been eternal after all. For anything that ends is only illusion and not subject to these rules. I should also note that as any part of eternity changes so does its complement. (See rule 5.)

These things are true for all things eternal. And though I numbered them as different concepts so you can explore them more easily, they are actually just aspects of the same principal. Take some time once in a while to look over each rule, one at a time. Look into every idea you glean from them. Explore what it all means in relation to your own current physical life. Only in the context of your own toolbox will these principals mean anything of importance. Be aware it is impossible for you, in your current state, to understand the total, comprehensive meaning of the axioms given to you. In your heart, you will know it is true, though it may never all fit in your toolbox.

Now that you are familiar with the principles of eternity, and all things real, let us explore illusion and how we can tell the difference between the two.

The test to tell if something is real or just illusion is very simple. Take the thing or concept you are exploring, and try to apply the six principles you just learned to it. Does this thing adhere to all of these principles? If it does not, it is not part of reality. It is merely an illusion created by reality for some reason.

Let us try this concept of testing for reality together, using some things around you. Let us start with something easy to test. Let us start with the book you are holding. Did it have a beginning? Will it have an ending? As you can see, it most certainly had a beginning. It was constructed by a publishing company for your use. It will, conceivably be destroyed one day, if only by the ravages of physical age. This physical book clearly fails the test for reality. It is only a physical object. It is only real in the confines of this physical existence. It is illusion.

Now let us try something a little more difficult. Let us try testing the reality of the truth in this book. Let us test the reality of the principles themselves. Do these principles have a beginning? Will they have an ending? The actual

22

words used to describe and explain the principle did begin somewhere, with someone. These words were created when the first consciousness decided to contemplate reality. The truth they represent has always existed. These truths will always exist, though the words used to define them may come and go. The words are illusions created to represent a reality. If you look, you are likely to find that all things in the physical world are not real.

You may find yourself asking, if physical life is not real, if it is only illusion, why does it feel so real? Why are we subject to all types of physical stimuli such as heat, cold, pain and pleasure? You may even find yourself asking why you cannot change the illusion of your physical life. The truth is, you can.

Your physical existence is so real to you, because a percentage of the energy that makes up your being has been transformed into a connection to the physical form that bonds you to this mortal life. The Earth is *real* to those living on her. This is meant in the context of a finite life in a finite world. To be part of this illusion called Earth, you have to become illusion yourself. Your physical body is not real in any other place or realm besides the physical universe that the mesh of eternity has created.

A piece of what makes up your physical body is made from the matter of the Earth itself. There is a code to all life on Earth. It is, in a sense, the sheet music to the song of the Earth. All things on Earth are made up of a compilation of elements taken from the particular sheet music. Your physical self is made up of segments from this sheet music. Without this, you would be totally foreign to the Earth, and unable to live a human life. Because you have conformed to the pattern laid out before you, you are subject to all things that effect that pattern. Including, but not limited to, physical pain and pleasure.

Think for a moment about the concepts of pain and pleasure. They are very real to you. They are a fact of physical life. Damage your body and you will feel pain. Pamper it and you will feel pleasure. Let us explore further into the reality of pain and pleasure.

Both pain and pleasure are basic physical responses designed to make you stop doing something harmful or warn you of sickness in the case of pain; or encourage you to continue to do something that is good for you or pursue relationships that are nurturing to you, in the case of pleasure. Consider this, though pain and pleasure are both facts of physical reality, they are not absolute. You can — depending on your state of mind — find something that is usually considered quite pleasurable to be uninviting or even uncomfortable. Likewise, you can control your physical response to pain, eliminating it from your situation.

For example, if you are in a sexual encounter you do not wish to be in, whether it was forced on you or not, you are not likely to take great pleasure from it. On the same idea, if you are in a situation where it is not convenient to feel pain, you will turn off your ability to feel pain until later. How often have you hurt yourself when you were very busy or stressed and didn't even realize it until later when the situation was quiet? As you also know, there are ways of using intellect to overcome pain.

So we see, even basic physical responses are subject to other forces. What is going on in your mind (your real self) can dictate whether you have time to allow pain or pleasure to be *real* to you. This is because they are not truly real unless you are immersed in the physical Earth. If you are not reaching out to the you beyond the Earth, and are experiencing a purely physical existence at the time the stimuli occurs, you will feel it. But, if you are communing with your higher or complete self, you may not even be aware of the corporal catalyst. When you concentrate, contemplate or simply think about something, you are communicating with that part of you that does not always show itself in your daily life. How often have you felt you were "running on auto pilot"? All of you, I have no doubt, have experienced the difference between being completely physically orientated and only partly oriented to the Earth.

The fact that any bodily reaction, such as pain, can be controlled and removed from a situation — whether you do this on purpose or without knowing — proves the illusion of Earth-life. If this world and all things that happen here were real, you would not be able to stop or start the sensations it creates in you at will. You would not be able to choose when to feel pleasure or pain. You would not be able to convince your body these things were not important, thus ignoring them.

I am not saying that your Earth-life is not important. No, rather it is the most important thing you are doing now. It is not trivial. You have elected to join in this illusion to help it come to its point of harmony. If you did not become physical and immerse yourself in the illusion of Earth-life until the illusion was more real to you than actual reality, you could not do your job. You had to get into the situation completely, in order to hear the Earth tones and understand the scope of the problems at hand. In that respect, you have more knowledge than your teachers do. We know what the problem is; you know all the nuances of the symptoms. We know what the disease is; you know what the pain feels like.

It is hard for those of us who did not elect to become physical in order to guide you from this end, to understand the way the pain has changed your concepts of the mission. It is often frustrating for us to remind you of who you are over and over again, because you are so lost in this Earth illusion you have forgotten you are adept and not helpless. You have forgotten that you are a master of your arts.

If you prefer, you can think of this Earth world and the physical universe around her as a dream. It is not completely wrong to think of material existence as a dream created by the mesh of the universe. The human concept of a dream is strangely appropriate in some ways when compared to what the whole of the Earth and its universe is.

If a dream is a reflection of what is happening in someone's mind, if it is a safe way of releasing emotions or working out difficulties, than this place is most certainly a dream. If in a dream you can do things that are not consistent with your "normal" life and can react beyond what is considered the rule, then this physical universe again qualifies as a dream. If a dream is a place where you may find yourself both comfortable and strangely disoriented at the same time, then you, child, are surely living in a dream. But if you define a dream as the visualization of a wish or perfection, then this place is a nightmare. This is because perfection is not the rule in this clockwork Earth, it is the goal.

Remember, child, this physical universe is just a place in the mesh of the real universe. This Earth is a node where lines of the mesh have come together and are not in harmony. Reality is the total of all things eternal and time is a creation of physical beings in order to put some order to the chaos of their universe.

Frequency of Life

When we examine interactions of the universal mesh, it is clear that many things can happen that will cause an intersection's energy to go sour before it can be tuned. The most common problem is a clash of frequencies. Sometimes the frequencies of the energies that merge to create an intersection do not agree with each other. When this happens, the discord can be tremendous. Some notes will not complement each other. When uncomplimentary notes come together, rather than working together, they try to overpower each other. By doing so, they create an abrasive, offensive sounding struggle. As each strives to dominate, all assemblages of harmony are lost. If the struggle continues, the invading tone may even overpower the original tone. This would result in an unnatural combination of physical reality and non physical frequency. It would be like forcing a tuning fork to ring flat.

When this contradiction of frequencies occurs, the energy that is physical becomes confused. It is no longer in tune with the chords meant for it. Though it may not have been in harmony with the total of existence at one time, it is not even in tune with itself any longer. This is what we have labeled *"frequency sickness"*.

Frequency sickness is a global affliction. This means it effects all physical things in a particular portion of a node, or in this case, a planet in physical space. Even in its most diluted form, it soon creates damage to the mesh of the universe. Frequency sickness causes the resonance of the energy that makes physical matter force itself to adapt to the new tone in order to exist. Depending on the interval between the conquering tone and the original tone, this adaptation may be mild or extreme. Everything in that fragment of physical existence is effected by, it without exception.

This Earth is, as you know, a part of a node in the energy grid that has been created in the physical universe. It is trying to find its tone, but it is also sick. The frequency of the Earth has been corrupted by several different sources. This corruption was not done on purpose and this corruption was not from malace. It was created by ignorance. The details of this corruption will soon be explained to you. Nevertheless, because of this pollution of the original tone of the Earth, very little of what is actually physically in place around you is as it would be naturally. Even the physical form you occupy has been greatly compromised by the invading tone.

How, you may ask, does your physical form affect the universe if what is physically around you is merely an illusion? This is a good question. It is also a very simple one. Your physical form was not designed for this physical existence. It is a mixture of the physical form meant to house a foreign tone and a physical form meant to house a native tone. If you were a pure Earther with no mission except to live on Earth and be part of it's natural, unhampered growth, you would be unable to do so. You would be useless to the cause, because you have the wrong toolbox. Likewise, if you were to exist physically on the worlds who corrupted Earth, you would be unable to fulfill yourself there.

Remember, your physical form is only one part of who you are. Actually, there are many planets of people in the physical universe who have learned to separate the physical from the non-physical, and truly use their body as a mere tool. Earthers, unlike these beings, have not developed to that point. Though Earthers are capable of mastering the separation of body and soul, the two are still tangibly linked. They are actually connected by an umbilicus of sorts that holds what is pure energy to what is physical. So, even though an Earther can exit their flesh, they can never really leave it behind. Without the flesh they cannot effectively interact with things physical.

I must take this time to remind you, you are not a true Earther. If you were, you would have no interest in what I have to say. You would scoff at any Master's words or simply ignore them. This is expected, and in fact necessary for the mission to work. You have to remember, this is the Earthers' world and we have come here uninvited. The Earthers have only one mission in their bodily life, that is to be a part of the clockwork of the Earth. Their goal was just to exist and maintain the tone, tuning it as needed, until they were once again in harmony with the universe. They were not expected to do this through any elaborate or magical means. They were expected to do this just by being a living part of the living Earth. They did not need, or even want to know, why they were living or what the ultimate goal of their life was. They would have naturally progressed to that point without intervention. They were meant to live and exist, adding their energy and their songs to the Earth, growing gradually with the world until their songs filled the ear of the universe. The Earth would then be in tune and the node would return to the mesh.

Alas, this was not the case. You and I, my child, are part of a race of people who physically originated on a different node in the mesh. Through a mixture of arrogance and ignorance, we contaminated this particular place. So why should they listen to us? We came and destroyed the natural frequency of their world. We overpowered their natural song and replaced it with our own, forcing their world to be condemned to suffer frequency sickness. We even took the key that allowed them to become a physical part in harmony with the rest of the node and changed it by mixing it with our own, thus making them unable to fully communicate with their own world and fulfill their responsibilities.

We are — in their eyes— still invaders. Though we have, in the time since we made this mistake, come to our own harmony with the universe and understand the great injustice our ignorance caused this world. Because of us, the Earthers are so out of line with the song of the universe, they are not even aware that we have been charged by our universal awareness to return and use the powers at our disposal to help the Earth come to her apex. Still, for the most part, these are problems we have caused ourselves. Trust is something that is earned, not taken. We have — in their eyes — done little to earn their trust. You must respect this difference of opinion. You should not force those whose orientation is purely earthbound to see your mission. It will do you no good.

There are several different sentient, physical based races involved with the corruption of Earth. In the linear time-line of the Earth, our people, child, were the first and the most destructive. There were many who came after us, most in only the last thousand Earth years or so. This has caused the Earth to suffer quite a bout of frequency sickness.

The suppression of the Earth tone, and the subsequent invasion by other tones, has caused this sickness. Its symptoms are easy to see around you. The easiest to see are physical sickness, mental illness and hatred. Other less obvious symptoms include competition, want and envy.

It is easy to see how a poor frequency match can cause mental illness. Think of your body as a radio and your mind as the channel coming into that radio. If the tuning is off, the channel will not come in clear. It may not come in at all. If your body was created to pick up a particular frequency, and your mind is not quite that frequency, you will not function properly. The messages the body will get from the mind will be distorted and confused. Depending on the difference between the frequency of the mind and the frequency of the body, the condition may be mild to severe.

Such a mismatch would not have happened in a world with only one main tone. Every person and every physical body would be in harmony with that tone. There would be no mismatches between body and mind. Everyone would be united together through their harmony to the Earth tone. They would be able to feel true community, and know the other's mind. They would easily be able to hear each other's songs and be compassionate to other's feelings and needs. To be cruel to others would cause a frequency disruption that would cause pain in all, even the instigator of the trouble.

You can see this in small ways if you look at the people of your world who are not as affected by frequency sickness. There are small groups of humans who have managed to do this. By obeying the Earth's will, and avoiding total submission to the invading tone they have remained clearer than most. There are Earthers who have never interacted with our people or other interlopers. Though they are not pure to the Earth's original tone — for frequency sickness is global — they are not as sick as the people in *civilization* are. These people use the harmony between them as a common way to communicate with, not only nature, but also with each other. You may call it telepathy. They call it knowing.

Mental illness is not a problem in these people. Why? Because their bodies and minds are in closer tune. In civilized man, mental illness is more prevalent and affects many more people than you think. Depression, aggression and anxiety are all forms of this problem. Most people experience these symptoms in waves, as the frequency of their mind's energy swings between the Earth tone and any of several invading tones.

Extreme aggression, as can be seen in the senseless killings and crimes prevalent in *civilized* society, are often augmented by chemical influences that cause the body to be further off frequency than it was when it was created. The negative emotions are often caused by the frustration the soul is feeling as it tries to struggle to maintain a frequency extremely foreign to it. Sometimes this struggle will take an inward turn and the individual will be washed with thoughts of suicide. More often, the frustration is directed outwardly, and violence is its outlet.

Chemical addictions are the physical manifestation of the body's need to maintain a strong frequency. In this case, it is the frequency created by the chemical effect on the physical body. Earthers do not like the mix of frequencies. Such discord of tones grate their soul's nerves, (in a sense) so most Earthers choose to listen to one strong tone. They usually pick one that is familiar to them. It is often the tone handed down from their parents and grand parents. They will surround themselves with people who are also trying to harmonize to that same exact tone and will consider anyone who deviates from it to be an outsider.

Sometimes, Earthers will choose a tone that is not familiar because it is very strong in relation to the tonal mix they were born with. A *one-strong-tone* theme is essential to Earthers. Regrettably, the true Earth tone, which is the only tone they should be following, is very faint in comparison to the bastardized tones developed over the years of contamination.

Influences such as drugs, when mixed into the physical body's structure, cause a strong resounding illusion of a tone. Actually, they block out the genuine tones in place around an individual. The soul's natural tone is almost always blocked out completely. This leaves the individual open to the influence of extreme discord.

This discord is usually constant and strong. The people experiencing this discord will often interpret it as a solid strong tone, thus adopting it as their own and focusing on it exclusively. As the drugs that induced this tone fade, the tone weakens. The body, thinking its soul tone is being taken away, will panic as the tone fades. This will create in the individual, a *life or death* need to attain the tone once again. This is what creates addiction and mental instability. This also initiates emotional dependencies.

Often, children going through puberty will experience bouts of extreme frequency sickness that manifest themselves in the form of mental illness. Much of the conflict between adolescent children and their parents come from the pure animal roots of the human. If man where still a wild animal, the conflict between teenagers and their parents (particularly between mothers and daughters, and fathers and sons) would serve the purpose of driving the adolescent to leave the human pride before he or she became sexually mature. This is to avoid interbreeding of family members.

This is quite a bit different from the effect of frequency sickness on adolescents. Actually, frequency sickness *kills* a large number of prepubescent Earthers every Earth year. As with all life on Earth, because of the intervention from abroad, frequencies in the body and soul of adolescents are not pure to the Earth's tone. During puberty, there are many physical changes happening in the body of the child. These changes, in themselves, cause frequency noise that confuse the child. Far more confusing to them, is that as each aware being becomes mature and capable of passing on physical life —by way of creating a new toolbox that can be occupied by another soul — they are suddenly aware of the frequencies in place around them. The simple frequencies recognized in childhood are no longer all they feel. These new frequencies are not natural. The more sensitive the individual child is to these changes, the more pain and discord they will experience in their souls. The new frequencies they experience, invade the stability of the ones in place, and if the strength of frequencies from the unknown overpower those of the familiar, they may find themselves unable to cope with physical life. They may not be properly prepared to handle this much frequency discord.

Depression and pain caused by this problem, can be overpowering, driving these children to release their hold in the physical world to escape from the pain. They, in Earth terms, take their own lives. Adolescence can be a very hard time for all children, especially those who are exposed — often by their own choice— to negative frequencies.

Exposure to negative frequencies does not end when adulthood is reached. Many negative frequencies are in place and very active on Earth. Some are knowingly hidden, such as those in music; just as we have inspired positive frequencies purposely hidden in music. Most of the negative energies in place around you are coming from your power lines, sub-stations, and even your television and computer screens. The energy they give forth is highly disturbing to most individuals. It has even been known to cause physical death. This brings us to the point of exploring the physical symptoms of frequency sickness.

Physical problems caused by frequency sickness are a little more complex to understand. As you know, most physical sicknesses are caused by micro-organisms such as viruses and bacteria. These very small life forms have many uses on Earth. They help remove natural waste from the world's surface and transform it into usable products. They assist in the growth of plants and animals. If you had no bacteria in your physical body, you would be very uncomfortable. They help maintain the digestion of food and are specialized to clean and maintain parts of your form you cannot even see. Even your blood cells are a cousin of these microscopic life forms.

If Earth were the ideal world — one that has not been touched by frequency sickness — these micro life forms would not develop to attack you. There would be no need. The Earth would not see you as an invader. You would be a healthy part of her. She would have no need to want to see you gone.

As you know, this is not the ideal situation. As mankind became further and further off tone with the Earth, the natural and harmless maintenance substances of the Earth became even more specialized in order to do their job. Since their job was to keep a balance of physical substances on Earth, some of them soon found it necessary to adapt themselves to attack the carriers of the invading tone. Since they were so very small, they attacked in the only way they could. They invaded internally, destroying the offending organism from the inside out, much as they would digest waste from the world's surface.

This caused great problems when our people first came to this world. Many of us died from sickness that did not affect the life already here. But eventually, our invading tone became stronger than the one carried by the pre-aware life on this world, and the micro-organisms became confused. The trouble became worse as we intermixed our own genetic material with the existing Earth life, creating a bastard race that was no longer in tune with Earth or ourselves.

Soon there were no life forms on the Earth that were not affected by the invading tone. Before long, the microorganisms that were once passive to Earthers, no longer recognized the hybrid Earthers as being indigenous to the planet. They were perceived as invaders, and attacked accordingly. As the Earthers overcame each form of microorganism's attack, the organisms would mutate into a new and more effective weapon. This process is ongoing and will continue until the balance is regained. Sickness of the flesh will exist until sickness of the soul is cured.

There are times when, given the proper tuning, invading viruses and bacteria can be stopped. This form of healing is something most of you can do easily if you allow yourself to. You may find you have the talent for healing others, but have a more difficult time healing yourself. This is because you are more accustom to your own frequencies and are more reluctant to change them.

The disease humans named cancer is a more complex indication of frequency sickness. This disease is triggered by just about every form of frequency disturbance. But by far, the most namable cause of it is electrical disturbances. All electricity runs in waves, as does your soul. These waves constantly pass through you from all directions. The more intense your physical exposure to these waves, the more you need to center yourself and work to strengthen your true tone.

Electricity, as everything else in this world, has magnetism. Unlike most things in place around you, the majority of manmade electricity has an alternating polarization of its magnetic forces. This switching can prove confusing to the cells of your physical body if they are exposed to extremes of this effect. Some of your cells may see this unfamiliar electrical signal as a sign to reproduce and change in order to accommodate the new signal.

Other times, these electric disturbances can cause the DNA, which is a physical coding of energy, to become damaged and reproduce a defective physical body. In some cases, a damaged DNA strain will cause a cancerous response.

Chemically caused cancer is very similar. In this case, the cells are reproducing and changing to match the invading chemical. Though it may appear as if your body is trying to kill itself, it is actually just trying to adapt to a totally new and inconceivably different situation. The affected cells have been tricked by an outside force into thinking the totals have changed. Sometimes, these chemicals can damage the coding of the DNA, thus causing the cancer. There is much in place around you that can create a frequency problem that will damage you.

Do not misunderstand me, child, you must live in this Earth world with all the Earth world inventions around you in order to get your job done. If the answer to curing this world were as simple as stopping all manmade electronic emissions it would have been done without hesitation many years ago. Still, it is good that you remember this fact and not put yourself at undo risk. Do not choose to live under high tensions power lines or on a chemical waste sight. More important than this, you must take the time to find your true tone and work on reinforcing it.

You will not be free from frequency sickness in this Earth-life until the time of harmony. You cannot be. You are an out-worlder in a not quite human body. Understand that you were aware if this before you chose to come to this place. It is nothing beyond your abilities to handle.

Healing this frequency sickness is a large part of the tuning of Earth. It is a problem we are entirely responsible for. It is surely difficult work, but it is our work, for our mistake caused this problem. At the time, we did not know what we were doing to the mesh of the universe, for we were a young and arrogant race. We believed we were creating life. We believed we were helping this world as we helped our own. It wasn't until much later we realized we were mistaken. We did not create life, we confused it. Although we did help our own progression, we did it at the expense of Earth.

The paradox of this situation is this: There is no such thing as coincidence or accident. All things in the real universe happen as they should. The confusion and problems this Earth is facing because of our intervention, and the intervention of other races, is exactly the way it should be. If it were not so, it would not be so, because time is not a factor. If we should not have come to Earth, we would not have. If we were to discover today, as I tell you this, that we should never have interloped here, "history" would be done differently at that very instant, and we would have never come. Remember, all times are happening now. Though time is a factor in Earth-life, it is not a factor in anything that happens in reality.

In your Earth-life, you may have found yourself saying, "If only I could go back in time, I wouldn't make that mistake again." I have news for you, you can go back, and you made the mistake anyway.

This concept may fit in your toolbox without a problem. However, for the concept to be whole, you must match it with its completor. Which is this: all things that could possibly happen in physical existence have indeed happened in some other off-shoot of physical existence. Every time a decision is made by anything with both body and consciousness, it changes the direction of linear time. All options of all decisions are worked out in some realm of physical existence.

Bearing this in mind, look at your physical life. Every time you made a choice, no matter how trivial that choice was, there is somewhere in the physical realms, another you who chose to do it differently and is working out the situation that arose from that decision and countless ones after it.

Who is real, the you who reads this or that other self who parted with you at that choice? It is truly irrelevant. When you are no longer bound to physical existence, you will have the experience gained from every decision and the consequences it held in your Earth-life.

The truly confusing thing from an Earth perspective is that these other *selves* exist, yet only you (who you are now) is real. The other *selves* can best be understood as probes you sent out to explore other directions of physical life so you may experience as much as you can from this form of existence. You are seldom aware of these countless tendrils you have spread though the fabric of physical existence. Once in a while, you may experience their paths in your dreams. But more often, you choose not to know about them in this physical life — lest you confuse your current concept of Earth reality.

Many of these other selves will be experiencing such serious disturbances they may even cause you to have unexplained feelings or dreams that are depressing or saddening. This is nothing to worry about. Though you can feel some of the frequency shifts these shadows of yourself are affected by, they will not change your original frequency. Frequency sickness does not work that way.

The most dangerous symptom of frequency sickness is the way it unites individuals who are afflicted with the same discourse. Remember those with like tones want to surround themselves with like tones. This causes all types of hate groups. The same frequency problem that causes one man to be hateful, causes many with a tendency to harmonize with his frequency to gather around him and do his will. The same frequency discord that causes one Earther to hate another will band people with like frequency discords together and war will start.

These wars may be fought over excuses such as land, religion or resources. Do not be fooled. The real reason any two people, or any two million people, fight is the same. They are afflicted by a frequency sickness and any whose frequency clashes with their own will be the enemy.

There will be times in your life where you will experience frequency clashes with other individuals or even groups of individuals. You may have found that there are people you meet, who you dislike immediately with no warning or preconceptions of what they will be like. Many times these are not due to strong bouts of frequency sickness, but rather mild clashes of discord. If you allow yourself to feed on this discord, you will strengthen the clash between the involved frequency and cause ill feelings, maybe even hatred.

Since you are trained to react to what your insides are telling you, you will probably find that you are more comfortable to walk away from a relationship with someone whose frequency is so contrary to your own.

Take the time to distinguish between frequency discord and feelings of the unfamiliar. Many times, you may experience a uneasy feeling about people whose ways are not familiar to you. This does not mean you have a frequency problem with that person. It only means that you and the person have different life missions. Exploring these kinds of relationships can be very exciting and revealing for you, so long as you do not loose sight of your own mission.

Remember that the Earth has a frequency of her own. You are here to tune it. You can only do that if your own frequency is as strong and pure as it can be. You have to listen to the song of the Earth, but do not be fooled into thinking it is in true harmony. It is not, or you would not be here. You have to dance to the song of the universe, for that is the true harmony of your soul. That is the truth of harmony the Earth is reaching for.

Lessons

42

Of the Physical Body

There are many questions you have about what is happening to humans and why. Many of you are experiencing encounters with different groups of people who are what you would call aliens. There are many ideas and theories about who and what these travelers are. Some of these theories are planned misinformation by human sources, some are the ramblings of confused individuals.

Your body, as well as every other thing that is part of Earth, is made up of very tiny pieces of energy. Each of these pieces is held together by a force you call magnetism. The smallest parts of physical matter, even the parts that are smaller than those that make up atoms, are charged with the energy force called magnetism.

No matter could exist without this wonder force. For it is indeed the key to keeping all things physical in physical form.

If you were able to look at pure energy from your current state of life, you would see that energy moves through all places in waves. These waves (or frequencies) cause a vibration. When a particular energy decides to become part of this physical world, this vibration (or tone) is an indicator of the form the whole will take in the corporeal world. What secures this energy into physical form is the force called magnetism.

To define magnetism in the form you learned in human school is to limit the truth of it. Magnetism does not only tie energy into matter, but it actually ties time into space. Without magnetism, this physical world could not exist, because this space could not be defined in time; and as you know, time is a constant in this Earth reality.

To explain your bodies, I have to explain the plan of physical existence itself.

As you know, the Earth is a node in the mesh of the energies of the universe. It has been created in order to work out a point or plan of Creation. It is a growing part of a growing eternity. You also are now aware that the Earth, by virtue of being energy in physical form, is just as much an equal part of eternity as any other part of Creation's energy, including you. What you might not be aware of yet is that the Earth itself has an aura and a consciousness, though not in the same way you do. The Earth does not think, dream or reason. The Earth is far to evolved to be so primitive in its connection to reality. It relates to the *God-force* in a much more direct way, since the energies that created it are far less likely to worry about making mistakes.

As we discussed before, the Earth is sick. Her frequency has been compromised by our presence. It has also been compromised by what mankind has done to her; not just in the way he pollutes and disrespects her, but in a much more important way. Mankind, through his need to exploit the innards of the Earth, is changing the structure of the magnetism of the Earth's soul itself. They are affecting the very thing that keeps the node in this physical reality. This is a foolish thing for them to do.

The Earth, as with many of the other bodies in physical space, including your own, have a percentage of minerals in them. These minerals are affected by magnetism. Many of the compounds that make the body of the Earth are directly affected by magnetism. As mankind digs into the body of the Earth, removing such minerals as iron, and transports them to other areas, he unknowingly

44

redistributes the materials that are holding the magnetism of the Earth in place — thus holding the physical reality of the Earth in place. The Earth cannot be a stable node in physical reality if the magnetic forces that hold it in place are not maintained. In the physical world, there are two poles to magnetism, positive and negative. In true reality there is a third point which could be considered the point where positive and negative come together and create a void of magnetism.

Every cell of the container that you call your body is merely a collection of smaller particles of energy held in physical form by the magnetic fields of the energy itself. This magnetic energy draws to it a more stable form of what could still be called energy. These are particles that are so small that they are really not matter in the normal sense that you would consider matter. These particles, if not held by magnetism, would be moving faster than light (which in fact many of them do) and by moving faster than light they transition from matter into energy. When held by magnetism, these particles slow or stop and thus are moving slower than light and transform to matter. Yet, they are still energy in its truest sense, only now they are being held captive in the illusion you call physical reality. Everything around you in the physical node is merely a collection of these particles drawn together in particular configurations to facilitate the growth of creation.

Since all magnetism, in this reality, has a positive and a negative and since the magnetic poles of an object attract opposites or repel like fields, it is easy for you to see how magnetism can put together particles (opposite poles to opposite poles) sticking them together to create larger pieces of matter.

When you align the poles of the material (not just the poles of the molecules, but down to the basic building blocks — those blocks that normally would move past the speed of light if released) then you have what is called phased matter. This is how your body can pass through solid objects when you are in the company of the visitors. In the last lesson, we talked about how frequency affects physical matter, and how frequency sickness can cause the body to become physically ill. It is easy to see, once you understand magnetic influences, how this can happen. For if a frequency disrupts the balance of the magnetism that is holding a thing, then the thing will be corrupted. In a similar way, electromagnetic fields will disrupt particles causing similar effects.

Your mind is energy in its purest form; your body is merely a collection of particles held together with magnetism. As more and more of what you call your soul or your consciousness becomes accessible to you, the energy and frequency created by your expanding mind disrupts the magnetic *glue* that holds your body together. This is why so many of you suffer the same physical illnesses. It is easy for those who do not understand, to blame those illnesses on the visitors you interact with. But the truth is, most of what you experience in way of illnesses such as allergies, circulatory problems, thyroid diseases, and other such ailments, are not a by product of your interaction in the way that you assume. What I mean is that the ETs you are encountering are not creating these problems in you directly. Though the interaction does sometimes trigger these symptoms. Let me explain.

As you interact with these visitors and with those of your own kind, your consciousness begins to expand and awaken. As it does this, it creates terrible stress on the body because as your mind expands, your frequency and energy level changes. Just like a high frequency will break glass, higher frequencies of your mind will disrupt the magnetism that holds the building blocks that holds your body in place.

If you take the time to talk to and interact with those who you call "abductors", you will discover that much of the work they do which you consider medical in nature is actually amendments being made to your body so that your flesh will not be destroyed by the higher frequencies of your expanding soul. Often, the process is performed in reverse and amendments to your body are made so that your consciousness has room to grow.

As you know, the growth of consciousness is the focus of the mission. More specifically, the growth of your individual consciousness is your immediate focus, for as your consciousness grows, it in fact helps eternity to grow. The growth of consciousness is an individual and all inclusive thing. Individually, as each of us grows, the eternity that we truly are *becomes* aware, and as eternity becomes aware so does the *God-force*. So you see, the amendments that are being done on your body are for the growth of Creation.

Many people around you will suggest that these ETs are taking your genetic material for some sinister motives such as adding your genetic material to their own bodies to enhance their own race. Others say they are starting a race of human slaves with the material or are planning to repopulate the Earth with human-hybrid, alien babies. Some even suggest that they are raising human children to be used as a food source. All of these suggestions are completely absurd. Let us explore them for a moment and you will see why.

The idea that aliens are stealing your genetic material to enhance their own race is not reasonable when you consider that it would only take one genetic sample from your body to have your entire genetic code and history. If this were the purpose, you would have one contact and one contact only. No other contact would be needed.

If they were creating a race of human slaves or human-hybrid slaves, then why not take adult specimens rather than raising human children which is very labor intensive and time consuming.

Many people — not just laymen, but many well studied people — believe that the ETs are raising a race of human/ET hybrids in order to replace the human race with these hybrids after some cataclysmic event which many believe the ETs will create.

If we look at this with a closer eye it is easy to see that this simply does not make sense. The first question this theory raises is where are all these ET halfling children and adults? After all, this has been going on for well over fifty Earth years. If every person contacted by these visitors were truly producing the number of children it is proposed they are, then there would be a vast geometrically growing population of human / alien half-breeds waiting to take over the Earth. Aside from the question of housing these beings, the resources needed to maintain and care for them would be phenomenal and unmanageable. Also, since the human male produces millions of sperm with each ejaculation, it would only take one or possibly two samples to produce thousands of viable fetuses from each man. Yet these men are continually contacted though their service would no longer be needed.

Another consideration that proponents of this theory fail to recognize is that these visitors already possess the technology needed to replace the human race, nevertheless they do not. If such a plan were imminent there is really nothing mankind could do to stop it.

Some have theorized that there is a secret deal with a world government or even some "karma-based" rules preventing the ETs from carrying out this "master plan." To believe this, one has to assume that either this government or some rules of karma —which do not truly stop evil or control actions— are so intimidating to these ETs that they stop short after they have come so far and taken the phenomenal trouble to abduct countless humans and raise supposed hundreds of thousands of hybrid babies to take over the Earth.

It is simply unreasonable when you explore this idea that any race or races would go through so much and be stopped by the words of a government which in this theory they are planning to replace anyway.

There are many other suspicions related to the consumption of human fetuses, but they are simply untrue. It is nonsensical and impractical to travel through time and space to attain a simple food source.

The reason these children are produced may surprise you. You may find this truth very difficult to fit into your toolbox. The simple truth is that they are another extension of the container of your soul.

When eternity divided and you became an individual spot of consciousness in the eternal time-line, you took on limits and boundaries. Those limits and boundaries were greatly restricted when you took physical form. As you know, each of us — students, teachers, children, angels, Creation itself — is an identical piece of an identical eternity. By expanding the area in which your consciousness can reside in this physical Earth-life, you expand the limits of how much of your true, eternal self you can have access to in this dream. You are adding space to your toolbox.

Because your body is limited to the amount of consciousness it can hold before it hits a critical frequency and starts to self destruct, other containers (some of which are better suited than your original human container) are created. These containers are not created with individual souls as your body was. These containers are maintained for periods of time, giving consciousness room to expand.

Because they are created from your own genetic based material and augmented with the genetic material of body forms that can withstand higher frequencies, they are a part of who you are. Thus, these containers are used to house the "over-spill" of your soul that you have access to, but cannot house in your own physical form.

Sometimes while creating these containers, a soul comes into existence and occupies the container. At this point, the material is no longer a simple, empty container that can be used to house others' souls. It is now a a living conscious being with a soul of its own. These are the half-breed children who live and grow with the ETs. Their lives are short, but their hosts and foster parents try and make them as happy as they can be in that time.

Admittedly, some scientific factions of some ETs have become fascinated with these hybrid children and have been working on ways of amending their bodies so that they can live longer and survive outside of a sterile environment. The composition of the soul is a focus of much of some ET's study. Many of the events you are subjected to while in the company of these visitors could be described as exercises to enhance or expand the soul.

As you know, there are many other physical procedures aside from the collection of genetic material to create consciousness expanding containers that are performed on your body. The reasons for some of these are very simple. For example, you may undergo a procedure where a tube like device is inserted into your body through your rectal opening. This procedure is done to remove toxic food matter from your intestines. Much of the food you eat, particularly meats, are grown with large amounts of steroids and hormones; especially in beef. These steroids and hormones remain in the meat in a broken down form which absorbs through the intestinal wall and enters your blood stream.

The steroids from the meat have many effects on the human body. The most prominent effect in men is to create aggressiveness. In too great a quantity it can even create a sense of anxiety which can manifest as paranoia or malice. Over time the steroids also — by way of creating chemical frequency differences (frequency sickness) — become carcinogenic in the body and hyperactive, mutated cell growth results. The same steroids in women create anxiety and depression.

Hormones found in meat, when absorbed into a female body over time, can create side effects such as over muscular growth, unusual body hair, and infertility.

In men they can create unhealthy sexual cravings, aggressive behavior, a feeling of competition with colleagues, and physical sluggishness.

The insecticides which are in your fruits and vegetables (that come from not just coatings that are sprayed on the vegetables, but also from the ground that the vegetables grow in) also have a wide range of physical effects on your body. These include abnormal mutated cell growth and hormonal and emotional difficulties. In short, things that are not in harmony with the Earth, when ingested, cause frequency discord inside the body.

This is why many times when you are in the company of these visitors you undergo a procedure with the tube device to remove these compounds from your system before they can damage you further.

Another common procedure in both males and females — though popular researchers seem to only think this happens to women, because they believe it is some sort of fertility test rather than what it truly is — is the insertion of a penetrating device through the navel into the stomach where cell matter from the stomach lining is collected. The cellular matter is catalogued and used like a finger print. As amendments are made to your body this procedure will be done again to verify that genetic amendments have taken root.

Of course, as you know, many contactees are implanted with devices of a mechanical nature. These devices have many uses. The most simple is a tracking device which is often put in the hands or fingers if the contactee will be moving out of a general contact target area.

A second device is a small object that is placed in the pituitary gland and the hypothalamus by way of the nose. This device monitors the endocrine system of your body and the reproductive system. Often, it is necessary to suppress ovulation in females so that the uterus does not cycle through producing menstruation. This is so the genetic material being hosted by the contactee, which will be used to expand their consciousness, is not accidentally discarded in the process. As a side note, often contactee women experience a heightened psychic ability and sense of awareness when they are producing these genetic containers because their consciousness has more room to expand. When women are producing these containers, it is not a true pregnancy, there are no pregnancy hormones produced. The container grows in a self-sufficient internal environment. It is important to remember when reading this that though these containers may look like human or human/hybrid children, they have no consciousness, no souls, no minds, therefore no life. If they were allowed to come to term in a humanly normal way, they could not and would not be born with *life*. They are simply cellular material in a particular, recognizable form.

It must be made very clear that if any of these containers takes on even the slightest indication of having consciousness, awareness or a soul, it is implanted into the host's uterus in the standard biological way to come to term — in the case of purely human material — or, in the case of hybrid material, would be implanted in an ET host —or birthing system if possible— until term. No life is ever taken.

The master implant, that being the device that controls the others and keeps communication with the ETs, is located behind your right ear — sometimes behind the left depending on a persons body make up or system. This implant has artificial intelligence and a sense of awareness. Many times, when contactees believe they hear a voice speaking to them that is not there own and suspect that they may be hearing these visitors, they are actually talking to this implant. All of these master implants are connected, giving a group identity to the experiencer community.

You may be surprised, child, to learn that implants have their own intelligence and even their own identity. In the world of these visitors, many instruments used have identity and capacity for individual thought. Even many of the tubes mentioned above have simple rudimentary intelligence. The very ships the ETs navigate are self aware.

Certain individuals have more than one conscious implant in their bodies. Sometimes this is because an individual is in the process of learning or becoming aware and the extra implant is there like a teacher. Other times, an implant may need rudimentary consciousness in order to disseminate information and act upon it.

Sometimes, if your body is sick, implants are used as a form of medicine or frequency adjusters to help you heal. Other times, natural courses are allowed and your sickness will progress. The choice as to whether you are healed or allowed to become sick is a very difficult one. In these matters wisdom needs to override want.

If I may digress and speak on this topic for a moment. When and when not to heal someone is a very painful, difficult issue. As we said before, many of the illnesses that your body experiences are caused by frequecy discord or the stress your mind puts on your physical form as it grows. Since your frequency is so different from that of the Earth's, the Earth's natural defenses, such as bacteria and viruses, may attack you more often. Many of you ask your teachers why we do not use tools that are at our disposal to cure you every time you become ill. Many of you even become bitter or angry with us when we do not cure you.

Knowing when and when not to interfere with the natural working of the body, including illness, is a difficult choice and is not made lightly. You may not believe it, but often you yourself make the choice on whether you want to be healed. This is not in minor things such as colds and flues, but with more complex illnesses. Illnesses that are terminal in nature are never taken lightly. Yet we know that to interfere in the natural life-cycle can often cause more harm to the order of things. It becomes a case where the life of the individual, and the wants of those who care for the individual, have to be weighed against what can happen when you compromise the time-line.

Sometimes this choice is made and the individual is healed but these cases are rare. Usually, when you hear a story of a person who contracts a seemingly fatal disease and is cured miraculously by intervention, the disease was misdiagnosed by human standards, or in most cases, they have cured themselves by adjusting their frequency — often done through the focus that occurs during meditation or prayer.

People are very critical of their spiritual teachers when it comes to issues of healing, but the simple fact is that we cannot make that decision. To heal everyone indiscriminately may sentence some people to reliving their life with even more suffering, because sometimes a persons terminal illness is actually needed by them in order to learn and experience something that they will bring with them into their next existence. By denying them the ability to experience this, they are condemned to experience it in a more intense form later on.

We realize that this is a difficult issue for you to understand. When you or someone you love is sick, the only thing you want is a cure. However, I must tell you, the strength that you have to cure yourself is inside of you. You can, by changing your frequency and visualizing reality, cure any illness; be it of biological, viral, or chemical nature. Allowing yourself to know this unleashes the power to do this. If you cannot heal yourself after you are aware of the power, then it is probably because your higher self knows that you are ill for a reason.

When you are in this dream it is easy to think of sickness and death as horrible ends. But in fact, sickness is another tool, albeit an uncomfortable one, and death is a doorway out of the dream.

Returning to the topic of your body, remember the following:

1. Your body is a vehicle that allows you to exist in the dream.
2. Your body limits the amount of your true self that you can be aware and access at any one time.
3. The forces of magnetism and frequency affect your body in physically real ways.
4. Your body is undergoing amendments to change it and evolve it into a better toolbox.
5. Your body is not permanent. Eventually you will return to reality and leave the dream.

One more thing, your body has a very special ability. It is an ability that is only the dream. Your body has the unique pleasure of being able to create new accesses to the dream, so that others can join you on this mission. This is a gift you were given that is meant for you to share.

Of the Spirit Body

You may not be aware of it, child, but you actually have more than one body. Your entire being is made up of a collection of three separate and distinct bodies and four states of consciousness.

The First Body: The Physical Body

The first body is the obvious physical body. This is the body that is created by the elements in this dream. This is the vehicle you use to propel yourself through this dream. Without this body you do not exist in this dream. This body is a tool that you use to interact with and perform the mission. It is your toolbox.

The Second Body: The Waking Dream

This is the body that some would call your astral body. It has been wrongly labeled the soul. It is not. It is merely a manifestation of a different type of toolbox that allows you access to a median point between the dream (being physical reality) and reality (being what you can perceive is a dream). This body actually has a physical substance, though the substance is not entirely measurable by your current instruments. When in this body, it is easy for you to see physical surroundings and sometimes —if you have the will to— you can actually affect a presence that others will see; or affect objects causing them movement. This body is permanently affixed to the physical body by way of a sort of umbilicus. This stops one body from separating from the other in a more permanent sense. It ties the actual thinking part of your mind to your physical life. If this cord is broken or severed, the bodies will separate and the physical body will no longer function. This is also the body that is most often labeled a *ghost*. Though sometimes ghost or haunting phenomena are simply echoes of passions or energies that have imprinted into the energy of a current place (thus leaving behind a kind of residue of their previous existence), sometimes ghosts are actually a once fully living person's astral body that remains alive after their physical body has died. Often, this happens because the person who died has unfinished business and they are trying to complete it before they allow themselves to pass. Other times, it is because they are caught in a *dream-loop*, and they do not know they are died. They may try, in vain, to complete some task or action they were pursuing at the time of their death. On other occasions, a person may be so connected to an object, that they will not leave that object. Just as in astral existence for the living, there is likely to be a distortion in the way time is perceived and thus the *ghost* may not be aware of any time difference or change in environment. They may even stop to open doors that no longer exist, or climb stairs that have long since been taken down.

Your living astral body is a vehicle of growth for the rest of your total being. But the ghost body is, in fact, by its nature stagnant in growth and should be encouraged to move on. This can be most often achieved by asking the lost, astral-bound being to recall to you the last thing they remember doing before they found themselves where they are.

Some of you may be sensitive to the presence of ghosts. You maybe even physically see them. If you have this ability, you could easily train yourself to see other beings who are not disconnected from their physical self when they are in astral form. This is a very useful tool for communication over a long distance.

The Third Body: The Body of Light

The body of light, also called the *absentenial* body, is more what could be described as the physical representation of the soul, in that it can be an actual physical form that closest resembles the self-image of the person projecting it. Though it may be hard for you to believe, child, the light body has no substance in this physical world aside from pure energy. Many of your teachers and guides —those voices that you hear which help you along— are in this form. It is not impossible for you to enter this form yourself, for it is a part of what you are. You may have experienced the phenomenon of *out-of-the-body travel*. Many of you experience it on a regular basis. You may assume when you are in an out-of-the-body state that you are in astral projection. But it is far more likely, unless you are dreaming, that it is your *absentenial self* or your *light being* that is venturing forth.

You may have wondered how come you can have memories of experiences where you are in your physical form, though you may not look entirely like yourself, yet you know that your body is safe at home. At these times you may wonder how you can be in two places at one time. You may be sure that you were out in the company of the community, yet others swear that they physically saw you that night. For example, you may awake with full memory of being in the company of your spiritual teachers, yet your spouse or others around you will be adamant that you were in bed all night. At these points, child, you may wonder if your experiences are really happening. You may wonder if you are really going anywhere. It may confuse you that the memory is so physically real, yet your physical form has been witnessed and accounted for through the night.

The explanation is really very simple. It was not your physical body, it was your absentenial body that was out and experiencing.

Your light body has an amazing ability. Because your light body is pure energy, and because pure energy can slip in and out of the dream, your light body can pass beyond the dream you call physical reality and into realms where the universe is more "real."

As explained earlier, matter is simply energy in a dormant form. In actual reality, that being eternity, matter and energy are indistinguishable and exchangeable.

Because matter is energy, and energy can be matter we can consider them different sides of an equation — different sides of a polarity. They are forces that are different but identical. Therefore, given the correct conditions, matter can become the energy which it truly is, or energy can become dormant and turn into matter.

There are many realms of existence that circle, cover and pass through the Earth. Some of these dimensions (realms) have a polarity like the Earth's, therefore if energy from the Earth enters those realms it remains energy. If matter were to enter those realms it would remain matter.

In realms of reverse polarity, energy would take on material form, likewise material would take on the form of energy. So, if your light body were to enter a realm of reverse polarity — *a realm of absence* — it would take on physical form.

The configuration of this matter is determined by the intent and state of mind of the light body as it enters this realm. For example, if your physical self is a very short, round person, yet you fancy yourself tall and muscular, when the energy that is your light being — your absentenial body — enters a realm of reverse polarity, it will take on the form which you see in your heart. So, while there, you will appear in the physical form of a tall muscular person. Since the configuration of your energy body is determined by emotional state and picture of self, you may not appear exactly the same each time you enter an absentenial plane.

The materialization of physical matter, other than the body, in realms of reverse polarity is a bit more difficult, though not impossible for one person alone to do. Therefore, only the most experienced of you will materialize in reverse polarity realms or places of gathering fully clothed. All physical matter that exists in these realms is merely stationary energy put there — typically — by some group of beings at some time. For when these realms are first entered they are undeveloped. Unlike physical reality, there is no material base. Thus, the worlds of these realms are created solely by those who enter them.

For example, it is relatively common to enter a realm of reverse polarity and find it oddly similar to the Earth itself, having trees, grass, rocks, houses, etc. Sometimes certain realms are more specific in their design, taking on a very definite appearance intended by those who develop it. Another example is that many of you may remember being led into a very formal, traditionally decorated, English sitting room or den where you met with beings who are obviously not English squire gentlemen. The beings themselves created the setting for the benefit of the humans, based on what they felt would impress them and make them feel comfortable.

Many times, when several community members of the same age group enter a realm of reverse polarity together, their combined experience of what they find comforting will define the appearance of the material surroundings. Thus, they may enter a realm to find themselves in a 1970's style shag carpeted playroom, or in a 1950's soda shop. Again, the decor was created from their consensus of what was considered comfortable.

Despite the fact that each has the ability to change their physical appearance on entering these realms, often times people will appear in very similar physical form again and again. This generally proves that each individual has a strong internalized sense of what they appear like to others or what they wish to appear like, and it remains the same over time. With most humans choosing to be tall, slightly muscular, light haired, and approximately 30 years of age; despite the age, race or physical appearance of their human body.

When the absentenial body enters a realm of like polarity it does not turn into physical matter and remains energy. It is a pure energy and an energy that is accustomed to fitting in and operating a physical body. In some enviroments, your teachers have actually created containers for this purpose. Since these containers have no owner-souls, the essence entering them have no resistance.

This differs greatly from the act of *channeling* which can be defined as one of two things. The first is the displacement of a being by another total consciousness. In these *total channelings* the host person will relinquish their body and allow another being to utilize their physical form. The second is when the soul of the incoming being shares or dominates the host being's physical form.

The three bodies together are all necessary to make up a toolbox in order to house what you would call your soul. The label which you put on the soul is actually inappropriate for what it truly is. For, in fact if, you stick to the strictest of human definitions of what a soul is, you have no soul. You have many souls. You are not truly an individual, but you are unique. For, you as an individual, are in fact one soul with creation and we know that creation is the total of all things. Therefore, it follows, child, that you are also the total of all things.

As stated in the beginning of this lesson, it not only takes up three bodies to make your being, but also four states of consciousness. Just as there are several manifestations of your physical form that allow you to live in a multidimensional reality, so your soul has several layers and dimensions. We can call them levels of awareness — they are truly increments of awareness of the whole.

The States of Consciousness

The First Level of Awareness:
The first level of awareness is what we would call dreaming, but what you would call living. This awareness is your everyday, human, on Earth, physical reality. It is your thinking, it is your working, it is your grocery shopping, it is your going to school. It is the awareness that the sun is shining or it is raining. It is the awareness that your feet are tired or your back is sore. It is the awareness that your dinner tastes good or that you liked that movie you just saw.

This state of awareness has many advantages, The first is that you can attain it at all is amazing to your teachers, for many of us have never or no longer can attain this level. Sometimes this causes us frustration when we talk to you. I am sure, child, you have had times when you felt that your teachers were pushing you too hard, without regard to the traumas and trials of your physical life. You may find yourself thinking things like, "How can they expect me to do that or keep this attitude when my car is

broken, my job is in jeopardy or the children are crying!"
You may find yourself convinced that your teachers just
cannot understand what you are going through. Some may
tell you that that is simply wrong, that they are merely
trying to push you past the hard points. But in fact, child —
and these are words that many teachers would be reluctant
to say — the truth is (in many cases) we are so far removed
from the world you live in while in this first state of
awareness, that it is hard for us to conceive of and
understand how the illusion affects you.

Of course, that is not to say that these trials should
derail you from your work, it is merely to say that
sometimes our pushing is not wholly because we know
what's best for you. We are not in the dream, we are not sick
with the frequency problems of the Earth as you are. We
can see point A and point B, and keep telling you this is the
direction to point B. Only you can see the obstacles in the
dream between points A and B.

The Second level of Awareness:

The second level of awareness is what you call
dreaming. Many of you may find this surprising, for many
of you feel that when you are dreaming you are less aware
than when you are awake. But this is not true. It only
appears this way. When you are fully conscious in the
dream, you are engrossed in illusion. The illusion itself
becomes so real to you that you may be aware of nothing
else aside from the illusion.

When you are sleeping and you fall into a dream,
one of five things could be happening:

1. You could be accessing your astral body and
   experiencing things on the astral plain which is
   slightly removed from the illusion. So it is not
   wrong to say you are reaching a higher awareness at

these times, but it is not the same awareness as the dreaming state.

2. You could be accessing your absentenial body and experiencing things in other realities or other realms and just recalling it as if it were a dream. It is more likely in this state that you are also reaching a higher awareness. In the places you would go in this state, you will often find yourself in a much more *awake* state of being.

3. You could be in the company of your teachers or others, and remembering it as if it were a dream. Things you label alien contacts can fall into this category. In this level of awareness your frequency is higher. Often so high, that you will only recall in your human, daytime, waking state, things that happened when your frequency was low, and have absolutely no memory at all of the more wondrous things that happened to you.

4. You could be withdrawing into your own toolbox and exploring the depths of your personal experience. When you do this you are truly examining pieces of awareness and experiences that you have collected over the years. You are reliving them and gleaning from them more information that will help you grow as a whole. This, in itself, is a doorway to higher understanding and higher states.

5. This is the actual state of dreaming. (The four listed before this that appear to be dreams are truly not dreaming.) In this state, your mind relaxes and because the physical body is effectively shut off and

not asking for attention from your mind, your mind is free to explore things of a non-physical nature.

When you are truly dreaming, you will be aware of things beyond the illusion of life, you will understand things that you do not understand when you are awake. Things will make sense to you that did not make sense when you were walking about the Earth. You may even explore and relive scenarios in your mind with a new understanding so that they turn out differently. The visions and impression that you get in this state can be so strong that they can change, not only the outlook, but also the actual substance of your human life reality. For example, people have *dreamed* themselves well from physical illness.

I am sure, child, you have had dreams about things that concerned you during the day, and in these dreams you were able to find solutions that not only fixed your problem, but fixed you problem quite well. Yet, sometimes when we awake from dreams, the solutions we discovered do not seem to make much sense, if we could remember them at all. This is because the rules of reality do not apply in their totality on Earth; when you were dreaming you had attained an awareness where you could think beyond the limited rules of physical existence.

The dream state can also be attained in other ways. A deep meditative state can also achieve a doorway or window beyond the limitations of physical. Often teachers may tell you that dreaming is the gateway to the universe. Being meditative then, is a handle to open that gate. In your physical life, for as long as you reside in the physical body, it should be your goal to maintain a second state awareness as the minimum awareness you allow yourself to live in. By this, I do not mean that you should constantly be walking in a dream, thus not see an oncoming car or not be able to complete your work and receive a pay check. For as we said before, we realize that you must sustain yourself in this physical reality playing by the rules of this Earth-life.

These details are yours to deal with. But there is a certain flavor of dreaming that you should strive to maintain. It is more of an awareness or a knowing than anything else. The dreamer is open to all possibilities. The dreamer feels without restraint or embarrassment all emotions, good and bad. The dreamer believes in their imagination without questioning before investigation. The dreamer knows the words "possibilities" and "opportunities". In our dreams we do not condemn or discriminate — not even against ourselves.

To be like a dreamer walking in this material world should be the minimum you wish to attain. So from that example, you can see that your teachers hope (I dare say expect) that you will strive to be aware of all the possibilities. To experience every sight, every sound, every smell, even those you find unpleasant; to feel all your emotions; not to condemn or be judgmental — not even against yourself— to create a calm in your mind that will spread through your being and create calm in your body. When this is attained you will be able to hear the frequency of the universe. When you can hear the frequency of the universe consistently, you will be able to see and know that which is beyond the dream, and then you will have attained the second level of awareness.

The Third Level of Awareness

The third level of awareness is a bit more tricky to describe to you. Unlike the different levels of the body, it takes a certain amount of understanding and vision of what could be to understand what is. The third level of awareness is one that should be a goal in your life, though very few teachers expect that any of their human bodied students will attain it and then maintain it consistently.

Many of you do not even have the physical ability to reach this level of awareness in your present containers at the time you are reading this, but you will in due time as amendments are continually done on you. This is one reason why we are working so diligently to upgrade and amend your containers.

As your awareness grows, your frequency intensifies in near geometric progression. As we discussed before, frequencies can be damaging to physical flesh if it is not accustomed to it. The amendments will help your body become accustom to it.

Assuming that the proper amendments have been made, including the expansion of your physical container — which as discussed in a previous lesson is done by creating satellite containers that are connected to your Earth based container — and assuming that you have attained and maintained a level two awareness, and are motivated to reach level three, it is possible that you may attain this state.

The third state of awareness is broad and covers many degrees of "being". Overall, a level three state of awareness is where most of your teachers are. In this state of awareness you can see clearly and consistently beyond the dream. But even more so, you see the dream for what it is. You can look at all things and all times and all places with an objective eye. In particular, you see and accept who you are and what you are (including your shortcomings and your strengths) without condemnation of self. You are not only able to hear, but you are able to actively participate with the song of the Earth and of the Universe. The concept of all times being now is no longer a concept to you, but a reality. Though you are still physically based, so you cannot physically transport yourself through time without mechanical means, you are spiritually, intellectually and consciously aware of anything, anytime, any place, just by wishing to be.

Above intellectual and physical awareness, is the fact that in this state one truly understands what it means to feel. All intellectual knowledge will be judged by heart knowledge, because Creation itself is in the process of learning and growing. As I explained earlier, growth comes from the emotions you experience, not by the facts you learn.

When you are in this level of awareness, you know that you are truly a tool Creation is using to learn from. You are aware, that to be emotionally pure and allowing yourself to feel and experience all things as they are without tainting them by wants, desires, likes, dislikes, passions, and worries of what others will perceive from you, is the only way that you are truly contributing to Creation itself. You are also aware that you are Creation itself. For all things are equal and eternal.

In the higher, deeper reaches of this state, physical reality can often be controlled an affected. It is not uncommon for beings in this state of awareness to be so comfortable with the concept of the "non-reality" of the dream, that they can easily change what is not real to them. So, telekinetic, transmogrification and materialization are not beyond their ability. Accurate clairvoyance and sharp empathic and intuitive abilities often accompany this state.

It makes your teachers sad to know that some of you wish to attain this state simply because it has benefits that you perceive of as being desirable to yourself, rather than as a tool to aid the growth of Creation. Also, some of you work hard to attain one or two of the side effects of this state which individually can be maintained, and then believe you have attained the state overall.

For example, in this state of awareness your vision or clairvoyance, is clear, well defined and reliable. Though, just because you may have a reliable clairvoyant ability does not mean that you have attained this state. In the third level of awareness you do not *see the future* or *know the future,* you *are* the future. You *are* the past. You simply **are.**

In the third state of awareness you can heal the human body. You can affect physical reality in such ways that appear to be telekinetic or transmographic. Yet just because someone is telekinetic or can materialize matter does not mean that they have attained this state. Many of you will glimpse this state of awareness in your physical life. Some of you will have passing periods of this awareness. A few of you will reach it and maintain it for the rest of your physical existence.

If you cannot maintain this state, or even if you never see it all, do not be concerned. To know that you are dreaming is more than most will ever know. Eventually you will awake from this dream, and all of this will be irrelevant.

The Fourth State of Awareness

The fourth state of awareness is, simply put, the heart knowledge of the knowing, the understanding, the being, and the awareness that you are indeed God. The fourth state of awareness is something very rare. Unless you are involved in this mission at a very deep and very intense level, you may never encounter a being or teacher who has achieved, even for the shortest glimpse, the total of what it means to be in the fourth state of awareness. Beings in the fourth state of awareness are no longer individuals. They are aware of all their infinite parts. So not only are all times now for them, and all places here for them, but all beings are them. They have the total access, total heart knowledge and total consciousness of all things that make up God.

All these states of awareness make up the mind part of the mind / body connection that you are. Even states you

70

have not achieved in this physical life are part of who you are, for you are only in this physical form a very short time. Remember, when you are in different places, your states can be lifted. Consciousness levels you cannot achieve yet in this human world are probably very common to you in your life beyond Earth.

Over time, you may find that people will come to you claiming to be a *fourth* dimension being, or a being from the *seventh* density, or other such thing. When you hear these "labels" simply push past them and look at the person who is speaking. If the label means anything more to you than words, look at those individuals the labels are applied to and think to yourself, "Is the label appropriate?" If they are professing to be *more* than you, look again. For anyone with any awareness at all understands that we are all equal.

Even more important than this, is when you start to progress and grow, you may find yourself wanting to put a label on your level of awareness. Your ego may compel you to say to others, "I am at a high-level three awareness." You may even find that you feel you must announce your self-assessment of your level of being in order to command authority over others. But I tell you, child, this is not necessary. Those you teach will never have to be told where you are. They will feel it. Those who teach you will never have to tell you where they are. You will know it. Everything else is just vanity.

You may not be aware of it, child, but vanity has many more dangers than just letting ego get out of control. Though having an inflated ego can cause blindness concerning mission, the real danger related to vanity (and a more treacherous slope) is that vanity often leads those possessed by it to believe they have *achieved* their goal and they stop reaching. This is sad since reaching is often the gift itself. A more subtle danger is that vanity could cause one to see the reaches of ego and fear it to such a degree that one reverts to an opposite state and hides their true colors and abilities, thus never fulfilling their goals.

Remember, you are a note in the song of the universe. You are a beautiful tone that adds to a unending harmony. Without your focused and tuned resonance the song cannot be complete. So to sing is important. To sing in tune is paramount.

Of Good and Evil

As you ponder the total of what an eternal universe means, and you consider, my child, that all things are identical in an eternal universe, it is only natural that you will have questions. The one that will probably give you the most trouble understanding is the concept that good and evil are in fact, by this standard, identical — as are light and dark. This is readily explained by the concept that everything eternal, thus real, has a complement that is totally opposite of the original. Since both the original and its complement are inclusively eternal, they are by definition identical.

Let us begin by examining this, when applied to the concepts of good and evil. When you think of things that are good what comes to mind? Take a moment and ponder this, child. Do you think of moral values, religious virtues, and idealistic motives? Did it ever occur to you, child, that these concepts are often culturally generated and limited to the culture that invented them? If the concepts you imagine as being "good" are rooted in cultural, religious or secular beliefs, then they may not even be real to begin with (in the true sense of what reality is).

What is good for an individual, group, or people, may not qualify as good when measured by the standards which apply in reality. For something to be good in a real sense — that is in reality — it must have an influence of a positive nature on Creation itself.

Of course, many things that you believe are good, are good by the standards that apply in a greater reality. This is because many of the things you believe are good, child, benefit your growth and the growth of the node around you. Since the growth of the node and the tuning of this point in the mesh is the focus at this time and place (now) anything that promotes this is good.

There are many things you may believe are good that, in fact, are not truly good. This is not to say that they are evil in all cases. It may simply be that they are tools that you find benefit from in a passing way in this dream, but they do little to benefit Creation. There are things that are good to do in the dream that is human life, that simply do not apply in reality. For example, because humans are limited by their physical body, there are many good things that humans should do for their bodies that would simply not apply in greater reality. It is good to teach your children to respect themselves and others in a physical sense. You do not teach them to beat, maim, or otherwise do bodily harm on themselves or others by impressing on them the concept that it is not good to do so.

Another example is as follows: You are taught from an early age that it is not good to lie. Yet, if you were truly part of the total of the universe and not limited by your physical-self, you would be one with all around you, thus you would not have the ability or the need to lie. Therefore, the idea that it is good not to lie makes no sense beyond the physical dream.

There are many things, child, you perceive as good that are intended to be limits and guidelines to aid you on your spiritual growth. Since you are a piece of Creation — a piece as large as, and identical to, Creation itself — your spiritual growth aids the growth of Creation. If what you perceive of as good affects Creation in any way that is lasting beyond the dream, then that concept is truly what *good* is. The confusion comes when we put self and what is good for self (in a physical sense) before and above what is good for Creation.

What may surprise you — and may even shock you — is that some things you would easily classify as bad or evil are, in fact, by their greater nature, good.

Child, as you read forward, please pay special attention to the meaning of what I am about to say. It is simple in words but holds a concept that can easily be misunderstood. But if you read and understand it correctly, you will find that it will answer many of the questions you have asked over your life.

So let me begin. Good and evil in Creation are identical. I have said this before, but now I will explain why. Without evil there would be nothing to fuel the need for the growth of Creation. As you know, if something ever stops growing it is not eternal, thus it is not real. If Creation were ever to stop growing it would not be real. In order for Creation to grow it needs something — some kind of catalyst — to give it incentive to move forward.

You may find yourself asking why does it need evil in order to strive for growth? Why does it not strive for growth with art, music or other such things? The answer to this is simple, but may require some adjustment of your toolbox to understand completely. First, you must understand that though the energies that go into art, music, dance and other pursuits of the soul are very real, and the reactions they inspire in those who are exposed to them are also just as real, the object, sound or movement are not.

When Creation decided to paint, the Earth was created. The energy Creation put into the Earth is very real. Just as the energy the Earth inspires in those who look at her glory is very real. Yet, the Earth herself — the physical matter that makes up the Earth (or rather the canvas Creation painted on) — is merely illusion.

The act of creating the Earth did not cause Creation itself to grow. What happens on the Earth as it searches for its tone in the universal song is what brings growth to Creation. You see child, whether it is a planet or an individual you are speaking of, Creation does not grow until the energy enters the dream and starts dreaming.

Ponder, my child, for a moment; who do you think will bring more in the way of growth back to Creation when they leave the dream and return to their eternal bodies? A child who is born, grows, and passes away from the dream never having to face strife, never having to struggle for understanding and never having to reach; or a child who is born, grows, and passes away from the dream, but only after a lifetime of struggle, lessons and reaching for more than what is before him at his birth?

Adversity is the key to learning. You may find this fact a sad one, nevertheless child, it is the truth.

Of course, there are many things we learn in physical life born from necessity or cultural exposure. These are things we "learn" in the sense that we did not know them when we began this Earth-life, because they are "dream specific" and limited to the physical. These are not things that mean anything beyond physical reality. The thing that truly matters is what you would call wisdom.

Wisdom does not come from books. Even if you memorized every word of this and every other book written, you may learn much, but it will do nothing to add to your wisdom, until you can apply these concepts with more than head knowledge.

Wisdom does not come easy. Wisdom is like a reward for surviving a battle. Often, wisdom is the reward for surviving a battle you have lost. In order to have these battles, so that you may acquire wisdom — thus aid the growth of yourself and Creation — there must be an element available to create an opposing force. Certainly, if you are striving to reach a goal that you feel is good then you would perceive forces who work to derail you as evil.

But I say to you, without these forces you could not grow, for you would have nothing to strive against. If you cannot grow without negative forces, child, how then can we expect the eternal universe to grow without it?

So, child, if in fact evil is indeed necessary for the growth of the universe, and the growth of the universe is the true good, then evil is not only necessary, but good.

This is not to say that doing evil things or giving in to evil ways is a good thing. Just the opposite. Evil is what you were created to oppose in order to grow and become one with Creation — one with God.

Evil in, its truest form, is something that aids in the growth of Creation by trying to stop the growth of Creation. The friction caused by the struggle between these opposing forces is also an energy. This energy can be used to create good or bad "dreams" that will often take on physical form. This energy, when put into dormant (or physical) form, such as in the physical universe, can take on a form of that one can label *positive* or *negative*. How this energy is used, and what it creates is commonly called *the tuning*. Let us talk about the tuning in the next lesson.

The concepts of *positive* and *negative* are not exactly the same as *good* and *evil*, though in common terms, the two sets of words often are used in place of each other.

If something is good, it is often labeled positive. If something is evil, it is often labeled negative. The reason for this is obvious. If something is perceived as adding to a pro-Creation energy, it is said to be of a positive influence, thus good. If something is perceived as adding to an anti-Creation energy, it is said to be of a negative influence, thus evil. In this simple context, one could say this was the truth. But, again, by limiting the concept, one loses the true meaning of it.

Positive is not simply something good. There are several things one could be describing when using the term "positive". Although these things could be considered good, they are not automatically or generally covered by the word "good". For example, positive is a term that identifies the generated force that is created when the energy given forth by the friction between good and evil solidifies in the dream as something *good* for Creation. It is also a name given to one of the three poles of magnetism that exist in the physical world. The three poles are the *positive*, the *negative* and the *nil*.

Nil, of course, is a point of no magnetism in the physical world — that point where positive and negative forces balance perfectly, thus, cancel each other out. Or, if you prefer, the point where they complement each other perfectly and eternally, thus transcend the physical universe and join with true reality.

An interesting detail to point out is that in this Earth-life, the concept connected with the world "nil" would imply non-existence. In actuality, it is exactly the opposite. By becoming "nil" in this physical world, magnetism indeed becomes factual in what is beyond physical —by that I mean reality.

Understand this, child. If positive and negative balance each other out, they create nil. Nil *transcends* into true reality. In order for nil to transcend, its parts must be non-real elements that come together to make something real. As you can see, child, positive and negative are not real, not in the truest sense of what reality is, but nil is. This is an important note.

Positive could also imply something that is moving forward in the growth cycle. If a being, energy or other consciousness strives to better itself while it is *in the dream* it is moving in a positive, direction. Notice I said *strives* to better itself. For, child, even if success is not achieved,

78

growth still occurs if effort is made. If growth occurs, then a positive direction is moved toward.

Negative, as you may assume, is the opposite of positive. This is true in most respects in the physical universe. Certainly it is true in the case of magnetism, as well as in the case of the outcome of the energy created by the friction between good and evil; meaning that if that energy solidifies in a manner that is detrimental to creation, it is considered to be negative.

You may assume, child, that negative would imply something that is moving backward in the growth cycle. But this is not always the case. Sometimes, pieces of creation — a conscious being — will choose while in a higher form, to return to the dream in a lesser situation than when it left.

For example: A man could be a great teacher in one life. He could understand and see the patterns of the universe and life around him. He could sense and be one with the energy of the Earth and God. He could, for many reasons, come back into the dream as a man with little understanding and little love for the world or his fellow men. He could have little in the way of attributes humans consider positive. If the being's intent is to be in a position where he will encounter more strife and challenge in his life in order to grow and aid to Creation, then what appears to be a negative direction, is actually a positive direction for Creation. That is, if in fact the man does strive in his difficult life to keep reaching and growing.

The above situation would become a negative direction only if the fellow did not try to overcome his strife and allowed himself to become bitter and lost in the dream. If that happens, he is useless to the growth of Creation, and has added *negative* influence to the balance of the world.

The balance between positive and negative is very important for many reasons. First, it is a constant, ongoing struggle. There is never exactly the same amount of positive and negative influences (or energies) on Earth for more than the briefest moment you can conceive of at one given time. If a true balance were to be maintained, then nil energy would exist and be maintianed and the Earth would not longer be in the dream. Of course, that has not happened yet.

When positive and negative influences cross over and eclipse one another, for a brief moment — far too brief for humans to measure — nil is created. If the dominating energy after nil passes is positive, miracles can happen in that moment. On the same line, if the dominating energy to prevail after the nil point is negative, then evil can have undue influence.

This is the only way that good and evil, as real forces, can truly do anything tangible in the dream. Otherwise, they can only make suggestions to conscious beings who are in the dream. Yet when the nil point is crossed, it — ever so briefly — opens a doorway (of sorts) to reality. This allows forces beyond the dream to have power over the structure of the dream for that very moment, and only that very moment. Which force will have the power is determined by the energy taking over the majority from the nil point forward.

If we examine this, we can see the difference between "good and evil" and "positive and negative". Good and evil exist in reality. Because of this they are eternal, thus, always in balance in the truest sense. Where as, since positive and negative are limited to the dream, they can be (and indeed must be) in different percentages in order to exist. If they are in identical percentages, they create nil and no longer exist individually.

This can be proven in one more way. As you know from an earlier lesson on the laws of reality, things that are real will seem paradoxical from the dream. So, with that in mind, child, here is the paradox about good and evil. As stated, good and evil are always in perfect balance. There is always exactly the same amount of good and evil in reality. This balance is unchanging no matter how much good or evil you can count. But, I have to tell you child, that evil does not truly exist at all. There is really no such thing as evil. Since evil is a force that causes Creation to struggle in order to promote growth, it is a good and necessary part of Creation. Therefore, it is not evil, but is a good thing after all.

Paradoxical, indeed. But even more so is this. If we stop striving to achieve good ends, evil would consume all and there would be no good, no balance and thus no more reality — no Creation — no God.

Fortunately for Creation (and for all of Creation's many parts) this does not, and cannot happen. For reasons beyond my ability to explain on paper in a way that you could ever fit in your toolbox, the balance of good and evil that are allowed to enter the physical universe (the dream) is always tilted in the favor of good. Yet, it is prudent to point out that the forces created by the struggle in eternity between good and evil that manifest itself in the physical universe is always alternating back and forth, between positive and negative, never finding balance except for the shortest of moments.

The time of this balance will come though. As it has come before, in this and other places. This time is called the time of *the tuning*. This is what you are here to do. This is *your* mission; to be a harmonic tone in a tuned song.

As you read forward into the next lesson, realize that this is yet another telling of *the mission*. It is not laid out in chronological order, nor is it for that matter, limited to Earth. Nevertheless, is it why you are here on Earth at this very time.

The Tuning

Child, volumes could easily be written about the subject of the tuning. What exactly is the tuning? In short, the tuning is a stage in the bringing of harmony between the node named Earth, and the rest of the eternal universe. But if volumes could be written about it, then there must be more. There is.

First, let us begin by reconsidering the concepts of magnetism. By now you know (from previous lessons) that all things physical are held together by magnetism. You also know that there are three poles of magnetism that present themselves in the physical universe — the positive, the negative and the nil. You know that the nil pole is the perfect balance between positive and negative magnetism that transcends the dream and becomes one with true reality. You also know that this Earth, and everything on it, is made of tiny particles of energy held together in their present form by magnetism.

You should also be aware that the forces of positive and negative influence — that being the physical manifestation created by the energy given off when good and evil conflict — are always (with brief points of nil) out of balance in this world and are changing constantly.

Although this almost implies that they swing from positive to negative like a giant pendulum, in fact, they usually change in significance, without the predominant side loosing its advantage. Other times, even if the nil point

83

is crossed, the energy settles back onto the side that held the dominant force before movement started. Periodically, the principal force will lose its hold, and the two forces will exchange places. When either of the last two examples happens, for the briefest of physical moments, nil exists as an influence on earth.

Likewise, the Earth, herself, has a magnetic field that holds the mass of the Earth and all that is on her in a static state — that is, their physical form.

The magnetic field of the Earth is influenced by many things. As you are aware from previous lessons, the energy that is being held in place by that magnetism that makes up the physical Earth is indeed a part of Creation itself.

You may have heard stories of "pole shifts" where, many say, the North and South poles of the earth will transpose. Will the poles really shift, Yes. The magnetic poles will shift.

Some mistakenly believe that this means the physical poles will shift and the entire world will literally flip over, causing the Antarctic continent to be on the top of the Earth. This is not so. Though the Earth may indeed wobble during this process, it will not be noticeable when you consider that when the poles shift, the whole world will experience a transformation.

Why a transformation? When the magnetic poles shift, they will — for a brief moment — become totally in balance, thus in nil, and the magnetism that holds the matter of the Earth in its physical form will be released. For a brief moment, the Earth will once again be free of form. As the poles pass each other and the balance is over, the form of the Earth will once again solidify and become unchanging.

If, during this moment of *nil Earth magnetism*, the force between positive or negative influence is also nil, the Earth will be re-created (repainted if you will) to the consensus of the prevailing energy that comes into being after the nil point is resolved.

In recent times, as the tuning comes closer (in a linear sense), the forces of positive and negative influence are becoming closer and closer to equal. They struggle back and forth, creating nil point after nil point. These nil points only last for the briefest of moments, yet during those brief moments, forces of good and evil are allowed to have actual influence in the Earth dream. As you know from previous lessons, the determination of which force — good or evil — will have the chance to affect the dream depends wholly on which force — positive or negative — takes control from the nil point.

The tuning will come when, and only when, the magnetic field that holds the matter of the physical Earth in place, and the balance between positive and negative both come to nil point at the exact same time.

At that precise moment in eternity, the form of the physical Earth, as well as everything physical on this Earth, will be alterable. Indeed, they must be altered. For once its form is released, it has to have a new form to take its place.

This has happened many times in the history of the Earth. Look into ancient times and you will see vast, seemingly overnight changes in the Earth's climate and life. This is one of the ways the Earth, as a being, grows and progresses. Each *re-painting* of the Earth's form is much like another period of the Earth's life; just as humans have infancy, childhood, teen-hood etc. It is a natural cycle for the Earth.

Child, you may ask, if this has happned before then why is this time is so different from all the other times?

The answer is this: All the other times, the beings on the Earth and parts that made up the Earth were all natural to the Earth. They all sang the Earth's song. They all were true to the betterment of the Earth. This is no longer the case.

Not only have we, ourselves, tainted the Earth so badly that the beings on this Earth are no longer in harmony with the Earth-song, in addition, the people of this world have lost the ability to feel the proper compassion for the Earth. They cover her with filth. They destroy her forest and trees, and worst of all, they have mined her belly.

You may ask why mining her belly is even more harmful than destroying her forest or covering her with filth. It is because of what they mine.

As you may recall from a previous lesson, when men remove metal from the Earth, (particularly iron) and they process it into other things, then relocate it in grand amounts to other places. Although, it may not seem to make much of a difference, it indeed makes subtle changes in the magnetic field of the Earth herself. These changes may be too subtle for human instruments to measure, but I assure you they are real, and they have had detrimental consequences on the Earth.

So, as the Earth faces this time of change, she not only is covered with beings that are not in tune to her needs, but she is also physically at a disadvantage because her natural magnetic field has been compromised.

Our people (your people) became aware that we were to blame for this. We became mindful of it not long after the last tuning of our own world. When our world tuned, it came as close to the harmony of the universe that an object can, and still have some sort of presence in the dream. We could see that if we did not correct what we had done to this world, so man eons ago, the Earth would have no choice but to tune darkly and become a physical representation of evil.

The form the *new Earth* is destined to take on will be entirely dependent on which force is victorious as the nil point is passed. If the victorious force is positive, then the world will tune to the song of the universe. If it is negative, then the world will be plummeted into an evil like the Earth has never seen before.

Remember, when the point of nil force comes into being, a doorway between the dream and reality is opened and either good or evil can come forward into that door and influence the Earth. When this happens at the time of the polar nil, the force that comes through will reinforce — with an intensity beyond anything measurable — the positive or negative nature the new Earth is destined to take.

To add to this perplexity, the Earth is a center point in a chain of events that has collectively been called "The Prophecy". Put in the simplest practical terms, the Prophecy is the biography of Creation — or if you dare, God. The unfolding of the Prophecy is the growth process of Creation. This particular tuning of the earth is a major step in a line of events that is as eternal and as real as eternity itself.

The *good* in the universe knows of the importance of this humble node, Earth. Be assured that the *evil* knows it just as plainly. These forces currently struggle over this Earth — not with battles of blows, attacks of force or wars of weapons, but by making *suggestions* to the dreamers.

By dreamers, I do not *only* mean humans, or those in human form, but other beings as well; beings who have no bodies; beings who once had bodies but are now ghost like entities walking the face of the Earth; energies generated by events of great pain or great pleasure that echo through the places where they occurred; lesser and greater energy eating beings you may label demons; and many, many more.

The actions and attitudes of the dreamers are the manifestation of this struggle between good and evil. The attitude and focus of the dreamers on this Earth, due to their rejection or acceptance of the suggestions, and how they work them into their own souls (do they strive for harmony or discord) are the stuff positive and negative energy is made of.

The predominant consensus of energy will create the basis for the New Earth. If that New Earth tunes positively, the Prophecy will continue and Creation will grow. If it tunes negatively, the Prophecy will be thwarted and Creation will die.

As you can see, this is not a situation to take lightly. This is why you are here. You, and those like you, have come here to help tip the balance in the favor of the positive. By learning the Earth-song, and striving for a positive energy, you add to the energy and force of *good* for the world.

We know it is not easy for you. When you feel that every negative force is against you, that everything that could go wrong to you is going wrong, realize that this is because you are important, and your positive attitude is important. To awaken your inner-self and find your inner song is important. It is paramount.

There are forces around you who know that as well. Although pure universal evil cannot really touch you, be assured it is doing its best to try and suggest to susceptible people around you, things that will hurt you or derail your efforts.

Remember, when you see this occurring in your life that you are the dreamer. You are the one in the dream. As explained in a previous lesson, you can make the dream what you want it to be. Given the right state of mind, you can easily re-write your dream-reality and surround yourself with people of the same attitude; as well as, protect yourself from those who would do you harm. Be aware, the most harmful of things are not bodily. The most harmful of things are those things that will pull your mind, thoughts and heart from your mission. Often, these are things your body finds very pleasant.

One reason, child, that you may be feeling an extreme sense of responsibility and a feeling of near panic to learn and grow is because on some level you know what I am about to tell you. That is: many of your co-workers — those who, like you, came here to do this job — have not awaken from their dream enough to realize there is more to their life than their big cars, comfortable houses and their money. They are not on mission. By ignoring their duty, not only do they make it harder for all of you who are working, because there are fewer of you to do the job, but they also, in many cases, add to the negative energy around them.

You may ask, why is there so much talk about "Earth changes" and times of flood and famine if the whole tuning is to take place in a instant.

The answer, once again child, is one that is not pleasing to relay to you, but it is not something you do not know in a higher state. The answer is that there may, in fact, be a time of terrible war, strife, famine and disease worldwide before the tuning happens. We, your teachers and yourselves, are doing the best we can to keep our *vision of a positive reality* in the dream, thus stave off any globally devastating events such as war, etc. We work to *suggest* to those in power, actions of a more positive influence, and try our best to discourage them from dark courses. But be assured there are those of an evil nature doing the same.

If the evil suggestions get a firm hold on things, not only will negative forces take over the balance of the Earth, but the terrible, apocalyptic visions you have been subjected to will surely come to pass. This is why you have been warned about them and prepared to face them — just in case.

Also, as the nil point is crossed more and more often, evil will take full advantage of any chances it gets to create havoc in the expectation of destroying the spirit of hope in mankind. You cannot let this happen to you.

There truly is magic all around you. Your Teachers, and your family in the heavens watch you and guide you. We support your efforts. We know that the job before you appears (from where you stand) unfathomable in its size and difficulty. But we also know, beyond a doubt, that you can and will accomplish your job. We believe in you. That is why you were chosen to face the challenge. Those who were the strongest were chosen to walk into the dream and save Creation.

When we were making the choice of who should go into the dream, and who should stay behind to guide, we knew the ones in the dream would have to do all, with little access to their full abilities, knowledge and strength. We knew they would have to don the burden of physical life, sickness, pain, and unexplained loneliness. We were also well aware that they would have to face all this with little or no memory of who and what they are. So how could we choose any but the most capable and strong?

As I said at the start. The tuning is something for which volumes can — and will — be written, but the truth is simple. The Earth is about to change. That change will have an effect on Eternity itself. You, and your peers, are here to help direct that change into something glorious. Your participation is not only required, it is fundamental.

You

Thus far, we have talked about the Universe, eternity and even God in reference to your mission. What about you? Who are you as an individual and unique part of the universe? Who are you as a cog in the eternal machine? Who are you as a worker on mission? Who are you that Creation could not progress without your existence?

When you look at yourself in the mirror, do you ever find yourself saying, "I am perfect. I am exactly what I should be. I am a master." Do you ever stop to realize the depth of how much you mean to the being that you would define as God? You should.

Each and every one of you, child, is a necessary part in the unfolding of Creation. Each one of you is no more or no less important than those around you. You are adept at what you are here doing.

You may find yourself asking, "What exactly am I doing?" The answer is quite simple. You are here experiencing that which is physical life. If you do nothing else — and many who have physical life will do nothing else — you have added to the growth of Creation if you have experienced the world around you. By using your senses, and your emotions, you add to Creation's knowledge. Everything you do, no matter if you perceive it as good or bad, adds to the fabric of what you bring back to Creation when you leave this Earth-dream.

If, in fact, you decide to wake and become more than just a dreamer, and begin to reach for growth and mission, then you do even more for Creation. But I must caution you, though you do more for mission, and thus Creation, you do not mean more to Creation. Every part of this Earth is needed to affect Creation's plan.

Let me give you an example you may find helpful. It may not be clear to you that there is any reason that so many children would be born into famine stricken countries. These children are destined to starve and die in a few short months, seemingly never having the chance to do anything to aid in the plan of Creation. But in fact, each one of them has a reason for existing.

That reason is varied and could include the following: For many people, seeing a starving child (or even knowing they exist) makes them more sensitive to the want and need around them. They apply that sensitivity to helping others around them, thus, giving that starving child a reason. Other reasons could include an issue the parent must face. Perhaps the beings who have taken on the job of the starving children have offered to suffer for the sake of the growth of Creation. Remember, the growth process is not just one of joy, it can be one of strife and pain. You must also remember, that it is not just the most prominent and famous (or infamous) who affect the world. You all do.

Some of you, child, have mistakenly assumed that spirits born into situations like this do so because they are paying a debt from a former life. The assumption goes like this: If a man was selfish in a former Earth-life, he will be born again into a body destined to feel the pains of starvation, in order to pay back a debt and learn from the mistake he made in the last life.

This is not the truth at all. If, in fact, starvation was a form of penance that helped a soul *pay* some kind of cosmic debt, then it would be wrong for you to try and feed a hungry person. If you did, you would be stopping the being from fulfilling its *penance*, thus condemning it to relive the same punishment, yet again. But, if you did not, then you are committing the crime of starvation yourself, thus, you would condemn yourself to the same fate as the original being.

How can this be? If it were how things worked, no one would be growing. We would all be in endless loops of payment and debt. You are here to affect Creation, not to pay a debt you made in this life or any other life.

Ponder this, child. When you leave this Earth-life dream, and return to Creation, you are reunited with Creation, thus, you are united in perfection. When this happens, you understand everything. You can see eternity and you are awake and aware to everything. You then realize that your previous *sins* were lessons you faced, and in some cases, learned. You also realize that the wrongs you did to others were inflicted upon yourself and your own mission, for we are all one. You find you no longer have the limits of human understand and acceptance, and you no longer hold any who have hurt you accountable, nor do they hold you accountable. You are whole.

If this is the truth — and I assure you it is — then when would the need for cosmic-debt occur? Why would you need to pay back your sins if you now know they were tools used to help you grow, thus aid Creation. Why would you feel compelled to do penance if you now understood that your actions — good or bad — added in some way to the development of Creation? You wouldn't.

You may find yourself questioning, child, what drives mankind to do the moral and correct thing, if there is no payment for sins. This is a good question, if you look at the situation from a strictly human-based mindset. Take a minute, child, and look at it beyond your human-based perspective. *You* are a living, growing, eternal part of

Creation. Your reason for existence is to help Creation create itself. Your reason for having problems is to find the strength and courage to face adversity and grow. Your growth adds to the growth of Creation itself. If you do not face your adversities in a moral sense and do not struggle to resolve your obstacles in a positive sense, then you are not doing your best job for Creation.

Since your only reason to exist is to be a living part of the positive influence of Creation, you must try and do your moral best to move in a positive direction, past your obstacles. If you do not, then when you return to Creation you will see all the places where you fell short. Your own disappointment in your effort will be much harder to reconcile than any retribution that could be brought against you by some outside force. If anything, you will want to go back into the dream and face the same obstacles again, so you can correct your mistakes. You would never consider going back in and wasting your effort in payment for an error. As your teachers tell you, and I feel compelled to repeat, an error means you need practice, not punishment.

Returning to the example of the selfish man; it would be far more productive to the piece of Creation he is, to return to the dream as a man with ample opportunity to be selfish again, consequently giving him the opportunity to examine and overcome his previous error. This way he can add to the growth of Creation. I must also interject that he would not be forced to come back and face that issue again. He may choose to. When he does, it is likely he will give himself additional obstacles to overcome, so he cannot only experience the lesson he missed, but also so he can experience more.

Note, child, that I said *experience* the lesson he missed, not *learn*. Remember, you are complete. You are not here to learn anything. You are only here to struggle to rediscover what you already know. The struggle is what causes you to grow. The reaching for more is the gift you give to yourself and Creation.

There are many layers of who you are and why you are here at this time. The first, of course, is that you are a piece of Creation taking part in the dream in order to help Creation grow. But why are you here at this node in the dream? Why are you here on Earth when you, so easily, could have chosen to be born some other place?

Normally, the answer would be because your soul-song is tuned to the Earth. You are somewhat spiritually bound to the Earth and prefer to come back to the Earth when you enter the dream.

But this is not the case with *you*. Your soul-song is actually of another world. You are spiritually bound to that other world. It is the world of the people who tainted the Earth-song so long ago. As you know, our people have been sanctioned, and indeed, mandated by Creation, to return to this node and assist in fixing what we polluted so long ago. You are one of us. This is why you are part of this mission.

Who are we, you ask. What is our name? Even if I could easily put it in writing, the name of our people is not important. It would only add to the confusion you have because of the of lies you are exposed to that are presented to you as "truth from alien races, or spiritual beings".

It saddens your teachers greatly as we watch many of the children we direct and assist become involved in a futile, useless game of names. They bombard others with human acronyms they have applied to us and other beings. Often, they even invent beings, as well as names for these beings, trying to fill their need to have answers. Most times, they do not do this with the purpose of deceiving, but they do it nevertheless.

We try to direct them to the truth, but often, between their ego and their intense need to help others, they seem to be unable to hear us, or sort out what we are telling them.

Many mission workers are so needy for direction, that rather than listening to their own heart-song, they read book after book, then try to force what they have read and what they know inside their souls into one reality. Frequently, this is harmless. For we do not care if you believe our messages come from a higher source or your pet, so long as you learn from them and strive for your mission. Other times, it becomes harmful when people fight between each other, each believing they hold the only truth. Each believing that what *their* spiritual guide, or alien mentor, says is more important than what someone else's says.

Child, try very hard not to let this happen. This is one reason why I chose not to tell you that we are "this" or "that" race. Even to give you a physical description of our former appearance would only cause you to try and apply concepts to us that come from other sources.

For example: We are not the beings who have small, thin bodies and gray skin with large eyes. When you think of them, you may think of many things. I have — by accessing the node and scanning the thoughts of a handful of you upon this writing — found at least seven names and seven concepts of who the gray beings are and what their purpose is. Of these seven, five are so opposed that the holders of those concepts would easily feel uncomfortable, or even threatened, by the others' concepts.

As I look into the node and access the minds of just a few of you, I can quickly see many examples of the misunderstandings going on. I see concepts of galactic councils, brotherhood alliance, interplanetary war ships, star armies and hundreds of races feuding and fighting for the possession of planet Earth. Even historical figures from your religious past using "star ships" to wage a war of astro-weapons above the Earth. None of this is the truth.

There is a Council, for lack of a better word. Its name is not human in origin, nor is it involved in the everyday workings of planet Earth. There are NO politics in Creation. Only in the dream can political agendas exist.

Anyone who tries to involve you in a political agenda is only distracting you from your real work. Do not let them.

This world is protected by us — those who watch it; and you — those who experience it. We are here to help tune the node and aid the growth of Creation.

Remember there are forces out there who do not want to see the growth of Creation happen. These forces are cunning and clever. They will, and do, hide themselves under the cover of "light workers". They will talk to you about love and the existence of eternity. But they will always make the mistake of trying to offer you some *human* level of reality to hold on to. Your co-workers who are influenced by these beings are "misguided". They are led — by the forces that wish to derail them — into believing that the mission is embroiled in politics, and based on wars of good and evil beings fighting over the physical possession of the Earth. They, and their "teachers", will direct each of you to be selfish with your love and understanding by saying your purpose is your personal growth alone. The message they offer is almost always one of SELF; not of the perfection of Creation.

Do not bother trying to change people like this. If you do, you will only find yourself, at best, frustrated; and at worst, angry and dark. Let them find their own way, for they will, because we are still working with them. We are still telling them the truth. Some day, when the lesser have failed them, they will hear us.

Remember always, child, that the reason for your being here is so you can aid in the growth of the being called Earth and Creation itself. You are to help not only yourself, but any others you can to grow. You are not on Earth to be a soldier in a war; you are on Earth to be a midwife in a birth.

You are perfect in Creation. You are not in the dream to pay any debt. You are in the dream to experience. You do not need labels to be. Indeed, if you concentrate on labels you will bind yourself into the dream and miss reality.

Be aware that you are a master. You are adept. The only truth you will every surely grow from will not come from this book, or from the books of countless others — it will not be handed out to you by some galactic council or by some magic, spirit force — it will come from what you already have. You are more than what you know. You have all the answers. You have the keys.

The Keys

Many of your Earth-based teachers continually request that we, your spirit-based teachers, give you the "keys" that will help you ascend to your own mastery. In fact, we cannot give you the keys, we can only remind you that you already have them. They are "in your pocket", so to speak.

But since it is our intention to give you the tools in these lessons you need to help yourself, let us review the most useful of these "keys".

Meditation

It is a simple thing. Meditate as often as you can on the energy around you. If that energy is not positive in nature, use your meditative influence to change it. If it is positive in nature, become one with it. Be mindful of the symptoms of frequency sickness. Take time on a regular basis to focus on clearing your frequency during meditation.

Self reflection

Look at yourself and your reason for being. See that you are an important and eternal part of Creation. Know that what helps you grow aids Creation. Find your strengths and build on them. Find your weaknesses, and with the same understanding you would give others, face those weaknesses and work to rectify them. Do your best to see your position in the team working on mission. Be a tuned note in the universal song.

Awareness of the moment

Be present to all that is around you at this very second. When this second has passed, be aware of all that is encompassed in the next. In this way you may *experience*. When you are not meditating to be aware of what is beyond the dream, then you should be making every effort to be aware of everything in the dream around you.

Feel and experience every sight, smell, sound, emotion — everything. Be aware of how you physically feel, the air pressure on your skin, the sunshine on your face, even the stuffy nose and fever you have when you get a cold. Be aware of your presence on the Mother Earth and her energy around you. In this way, you will become accustomed to the true Earth-song, and be more able to do your mission when the time of tuning comes.

Remember, your understanding and resonance with the true Earth-song is one of the tools you will need when it is time to complete our mission on Earth.

Compassion

Though the greatest gift is love, the greatest key is compassion. Compassion is the strongest of all keys to assist you in your Earth mission. With true compassion, you cannot be hurtful or evil. When you treat yourself and others with compassion, what is truly good for growth is put before selfishness, wants and desires. When you look at the world with compassion, you will be able to do what is right for this mission Earth.

Patience

Do not expect perfection from yourself and your world in a moment. The Earth, and indeed the Universe itself, runs on a time schedule your physical body could never understand. What seems like a moment away, could be quiet a bit further. It does not mean that it is not coming. Be patient, all seasons of Creation will come in due time. Remember, you are an eternal being. You have the *time* to wait.

Love

Allow yourself to experience unconditional love. Do not just love something because it is beautiful. Do not just love something because it is powerful. Do not just love something because it loves you. Love everything for no reason at all. You should not have to have a reason to love. Only when you can love without reason, are you, in reality, experiencing love at all.

The things above are the keys you need to become aware of who you are, and what you are to do, in the master plan of the universe. You need nothing else.

You may find yourself wondering why such things as "psychic energy", "universal consciousness", or "spiritual awareness" are not among the keys. This is because they are not necessary to begin. They are not basic tools. Rather, they are results of using the six keys listed above, consistently and in a positive manner. Once you have mastered the keys above, the "tools" you believe you need to get your mission done will come to you. When they do, you will realize that they are extras that can make your mission easier.

If you have the tools before you have the keys, then you may find that they can be more hampering and harmful than beneficial; for they can easily distract.

Once again, I must remind, you are complete and whole. You have these keys in you, you must choose to use them. You have made no mistakes, and you will not make any so long as you focus on a positive direction. You are a part of Creation. Creation is the focus.

Questions

I will address some of the more common questions you have. If you, child, as an individual, are already aware of these answers, please bare with me for those who are not.

You said that the Universe is eternal, if that is so, than what is the "big bang"?

Child, you must not confuse the physical universe with the greater universal reality. The physical universe only gives the appearance of being eternal. It is not. Mankind has not yet developed the technology to see its limits. The *big bang* that many believe started the physical universe is simply another point where energy (that is eternal) became matter (which is not eternal).

You said that Creation is truly real and is eternal. Yet, you said that if we allow evil to take over and stop the growth of Creation, it will die. How can this be?

This is another paradox. As I said before, most eternal truths will appear to be paradoxical to you from the dream. Creation cannot end. It is eternal. Therefore, it cannot die. Nevertheless, it is also true that if there were nothing to struggle against, or no one to struggle against it, (namely, no evil and no good to overcome it) then Creation itself would stop growing and cease to exist. We know that this is impossible by the very fact that we exist.

Creation will always exist, because if it at any point in the existence of Creation (in all of eternity) it stopped growing, it would no longer be. Since it is not limited by linear time, (as you recall, all times are now) the moment it stopped growing would be now. We are here now, thus, Creation exists. This also proves that not only do we never give up the struggle to keep good in balance over evil, but that we always succeed.

When we die, do we go to heaven?

If your concept of heaven is a place where you are reunited with perfection, your friends and loved ones, and are happy; then yes, there is a heaven. If your concept is the dominant concept of a land of "milk and honey" where there are houses and trees and roads like here in the dream; then no there is not. I am sorry to say that reality does not resemble this life at all. Remember, this is a dream.

Is there anything I can do to keep evil away from me?

Yes. Keep focused on the keys. Especially be mindful of compassion. Meditate and focus on connection with perfection. There is really no thing — no object — you can hold or carry to keep evil away from you. Yet, if you feel that a particular object helps you keep focused on the positive and on light, then by all means, keep that object close to you. All the while, remember that it is *you* and not the object that is making the difference. You have the power, the energy and intent to surround yourself with the energy you wish.

If there is some kind of prophecy, then does man really have freewill?

Though this can appear to be another paradox, all conscious beings have freewill regardless of the fact that the course they will choose is all ready known and recorded. But the paradox is merely illusion. Let me explain.

Since you live in linear time, you must see one moment coming after another in a set fashion. But in reality, all moments happen at the same time. When you make a decision, it is recorded in the memory of Creation, thus in the prophecy. That moment in eternity is *now*, but that moment in linear time happened a long time ago. Perhaps paradoxically, if you decide to do something different from what is written in the prophecy, the writing in the prophecy would change. Yet this never happens. You cannot choose to do other than what is written. If you did, the prophecy would reflect your new actions, and once again, what you did would be what has been recorded since the beginning of linear time. Your spirit teachers understand that this difference between reality and linear time can become confusing.

It is worth mentioning again, that no matter what you choose, all the choices are played out in other realms of the dream. These other realms are not in the *correct* time-line, thus do not appear in the Prophecy. This is one way of knowing these time-lines are not the correct ones, nor are they the one you are currently living in. (See lesson 4.)

If we are all identical in Creation, does that mean I am united with Adolph Hitler or other people who committed atrocities?

The truth is, yes. We are all one. Even evil people, or people who do evil things, are part of one Creation. For that matter, evil itself is part of Creation.

Does this mean that you are *like* Adolph Hitler. No. You are unique. You all enter the dream with the same potential for good or evil (or more correctly stated, postive or negative). It is what you decide to do with the focus of eternity that *you* are, that makes you unique. The forces you allow to suggest and influence you, and the degree by which you allow yourself to be affected by frequency sickness also influences the way you will live your life. Some people allow themselves — for many reasons — to be influenced by darkness and negative forces. Although it is not something pleasant, it does offer each of you the opportunity to stand up and refuse to allow evil to spread.

What is a sad reflection on humanity about the success of Hitler (and so many others like him) is not that he, as an individual, was evil, but rather that his frequency was allowed to spread across the face of the world. In fact, it became quite the norm to give into it or simply turn a blind eye to it.

So long as you do not give in to discordant frequency trends, you have no need to fear becoming like those mentioned above.

If the purpose of life is to struggle, is there any hope for happiness in this life, and still be on mission?

Child, struggling does not always have to be physical pain and suffering. Your struggle to wake and work on mission can be a very beautiful and enjoyable thing. Your search for yourself could take you into the world of art and beauty. Your search for the Earth-song will take you into the nature and arms of the Mother Earth.

It may surprise you, child, to find out that one of the hardest struggles you will likely face is that of remaining on mission when you are so happy with your Earth-life that you easily forget you are here for more than just the pleasures of physical life.

But know, my child, that your teachers are likely to assist you through your hard times and help you keep on mission.

After the Earth tunes, what will it be like?

That is entirely up to you. You are the authors of this dream. You will decide the course of Creation. That is why you are here.

If you take nothing else from these lessons, take this, "No one is more suited for your job, than you."

Be good to each other.
Alex

Notes

Notes

For more information on this and other
Sweetgrass Press books and authors visit:

http://www.sweetgrasspress.com

or

Email: info@sweetgrasspress.com

You can write to Michelle:

Michelle LaVigne Wedel
C/O Sweetgrass Press
P.O. Box 1862
Merrimack, NH 03054

Email to:

mwedel@sweetgrasspress.com

*Please note: Alex does not answer letters or take
requests.*

CPSIA information can be obtained
at www.ICGtesting.com
Printed in the USA
LVHW022252121118
596825LV00006B/406/P